German Men Sit Down To Pee
& Other Insights Into German Culture

Niklas Frank & James Cave

ABOUT THE AUTHORS

Niklas Frank (Real life German - The guy behind the concept)

Niklas is originally from Germany and has lived in several countries including Sweden and China. After working for a number of international teams at several companies, he realised that his colleagues were intrigued by some of the 'German' things he did. Seeing that people were curious about German culture, he started putting together ideas for a handbook to German culture.

James Cave (Irishman in Berlin - The guy behind the keyboard)

Originally from Ireland, James is a freelance writer who has spent time living in Berlin. As a non-native, his outsider's perspective meant he was able to see how life in Germany is different, confusing, and often unintentionally amusing to newcomers. While living in Germany he probably broke every single one of the rules mentioned in this book but, thankfully, he's now able to put all of that down to research.

Illustrations

Internal illustrations by Will Dinski (www.willdinski.com). Will is an illustrator and cartoonist living in Minneapolis, USA. He is best known for his graphic novel Fingerprints.

Cover design by Bruno Reis Santos (www.behance.net/lordmantraste). Bruno is a freelance graphic designer and illustrator, based in Portugal.

TABLE OF CONTENTS

INTRO

Every culture is subject to stereotyping, but few are put into a box quite as much as the Germans are. Ask people to describe the Germans and most will respond with a cliché: they're efficient, they're punctual, they have no sense of humour...

The problem with stereotypes (one of the problems, anyway) is that they're limiting. It's true: Germans can be exceptionally punctual. But if all of German culture could be reduced to a one-word cliché, Germany would be an incredibly boring place.

It obviously isn't. Every year, millions of tourists visit Germany. One would imagine they're drawn to something other than its reputation for efficiency and punctuality. Others come here for work or study placements. And many of those tourists, professionals, and students enjoy their time in Germany so much that they end up moving here permanently, buying a Volkswagen, and naming their children Fritz and Heidi.

Regardless of whether you're visiting a new country for a weekend or moving there permanently, one of the most important (but often hardest) things to do is figuring out what makes life there different to life where you come from. Firstly, it gives you a sense of the culture and, secondly, it means you'll avoid making any awkward cultural faux pas.
Most countries leave you to work this out by trial and error but since one of us is German (and the other has already been through the process), we did the most German thing possible and produced a guidebook to German culture.

Over the course of this book, we'll look at fifty 'rules' or insights into German culture. Why, for example, when the sun comes out it's completely acceptable to lie naked in the middle of a public park, but mow your lawn fully clothed on a Sunday and you'll get an earful from your neighbour.

It goes without saying that these rules and insights are generalisations. Not everybody loves David Hasselhoff, waits patiently at the traffic lights, or gets excited about the start of asparagus season. It's rumoured that there are even a few unpunctual Germans.

Stay in Germany for long enough, though, and you'll see all of these rules in action at some point or another.

If you're moving to Germany, we hope this book will help you settle in faster and easier. If you're just visiting for a few days, hopefully it'll enrich your time here and mean your knowledge of German culture won't be limited to just Currywurst and beer.

Nik & James

Basic Rules

1
ALWAYS FOLLOW THE RULES

Officially, the first rule of being German is to always follow the rules. It may be a stereotype but like most stereotypes there's definitely some truth to it. From a German perspective, rules are there for a reason. It's not necessary to always know the reasoning behind the rule or even to agree with it. What's important is that rules are followed and are followed at all times.

You'll see this obedience in action if you try to cross a road in Germany while there's a red man (or a red woman in the most politically correct parts of Germany). We all know the rules here: a green man means it's safe to cross, and a red man means that you should wait. Of course, we've all broken this rule once or twice, maybe even once or twice in the past week.

Germans wait for the green man. Even if it's 2 am and there's not a single car on the road. Even if it's pouring with rain and they're running late for a very important meeting. Even if the girl of their dreams is across the road, about to step onto a long-distance bus and out of their lives forever. The reason doesn't matter, following the rules does, and so Germans wait for the green man. At least, as long as there's someone else standing at the traffic lights or walking nearby.

If someone sees you cross the road when there's a red man you'll face the consequences. We're not talking about jaywalking fines here, although the Ordnungsamt (Ministry of order) do dish them out from time to time. We're talking about getting a loud tut-tut or even a telling off from all of the other people who are obediently waiting for the light to turn green. In extreme cases, someone might even take the time to chase you down the street (once the light has changed, of course) and give you a lecture about road safety. Germans, as you'll discover, can be very shy. But if they see someone else break a rule like not waiting for the green man all of that shyness quickly disappears.

Whether you're in Germany for a short trip or you're making a more permanent move, remember, always follow the rules. After all, they're there for a reason. More importantly, nobody wants a public reprimanding from a fellow law-abiding citizen.

2
LOVE BUREAUCRACY

Let's be honest, nobody really loves bureaucracy, not even the Germans. You might even be surprised to learn that bureaucracy exists in a country with such a reputation for efficiency, but it does. And even though Germans can be very vocal in their dislike for bureaucracy, in practice they're fairly tolerant of it.

After all, what is bureaucracy but a collection of rules? As we've already learned, from a German perspective rules are a good thing. Some might even say a great thing. Bureaucracy may not be perfect, and inevitably it always ends up becoming unnecessarily excessive, but it's much better than the alternative: not having enough rules!

A good example of the extremes German bureaucracy is taken to comes from an alleged Deutsche Post memo. It states:

"A postman's sack is a bag, which, due to the fact that it serves as a tool for delivering mail, is not referred to as a postman's bag but as a postman's sack, since its content actually consists of several bags."

Unfortunately, bureaucracy and confusing memos aren't limited to government departments either. Restaurants in Bavaria, for example, have a limit on how much shade their awning is allowed to provide the pavement outside. If a government official stops by with his ruler and sees that the restaurant is excessively shading the pavement, the restaurant will be required to pay a 'shade fee'.

You may not be planning to open a restaurant in Bavaria, or to become a German postal worker either, but if you plan to live in Germany, you'll need to deal with both bureaucracy and paperwork from the moment you arrive until the moment you leave. In fact, there are even forms to fill in when you arrive (Anmeldung) and when you leave (Abmeldung).

All of the paperwork might not make a lot of sense, and you might find the red tape excessive, but remember, all of this is a quintessential part of what it means to be German. More importantly it's a rite of passage for anyone that wants a genuine experience of German culture, and for anyone who wants to be able to say that they lived in Germany and survived to tell the tale!

3
HAVE A GOOD SENSE OF HUMOUR

The myth that Germans don't have a sense of humour is exactly that, a myth. Germans do have a sense of humour. Not all of them, and it may not be the same as yours, but Germans are definitely able to both crack and appreciate a joke.

The fact the world thinks that Germans don't have a sense of humour shouldn't come as a surprise. It's a stereotype that we've all grown up hearing. Those WWII movies featuring angry, goose-stepping Germans don't exactly paint them to be a barrel of laughs either.

But the real reason that this stereotype has persisted is because to understand German humour, you need to speak German. And, despite some of us having even tried to learn it in school, most of us don't.

If you have already mastered the German language, you might be tempted to go to a German comedy club to see this mysterious sense of humour for yourself. Unfortunately, it isn't quite that easy as stand-up comedy isn't as commonplace in Germany as it is in other countries. The closest thing to it is Kabarett, which is also one of the furthest things from it. The jokes in Kabarett tend to be fairly high-brow, irreverent, and often quite dark - a world apart from jokes about the differences between the sexes, smoking weed, and masturbation. In Germany subtle, intellectual jokes that require you to be incredibly up-to-date on that week's German news tend to go over well, whereas broader, mainstream jokes will barely register a smile.

This means that the best German jokes are rarely, if ever, worth translating into other languages. Even people who have been living in Germany for many years and are fairly well-informed about current events struggle to understand all of the jokes. Wordplay, in particular, makes it difficult for non-natives to understand the subtext that makes a bog-standard joke thigh-slappingly hilarious to a group of Germans. In short, you'll have to take them at their word when they say they genuinely do have a funny bone.

E.B. White famously said that "analyzing humor is a bit like dissecting a frog". You learn how it works but the thing dies in the process. Given that translating German humour to the rest of the world would not only require subtitles but additional explanations as well, it's no surprise that German humour hasn't found much of an international audience. The only German humour that's really made its way into English-speaking culture is April Fool's Day, which is said to have originated in Germany.

As with the rest of the world, April Fool's Day is a day for people to prank each other. Pranking in this sense doesn't mean putting clingfilm on the toilet or shaving off someone else's eyebrows. Germans prefer the more traditional April fool's jokes, like fake newspaper stories. In particular, stories about increased levels of bureaucracy tend to go down particularly well as seems to be the case with these two 'hilarious' stories from 2015.

Mecklenburg-Western Pomerania, Germany: The German Wild Animals Foundation has announced that they are going to install security cameras in the forests of Mecklenburg-Western Pomerania. Anyone caught breaking any of the forest rules will be reported to the local police.

Hesse, Germany: Kassel's transport company KVG announced that they now have sniffer dogs capable of sniffing out people travelling without a ticket. The dogs can do this by picking up on hormones released through nervous sweating.

April Fool's jokes aside, Germans do have a good and usually very dry sense of humour and in social situations you'll find them just as likely as non-Germans to crack a joke, if not more so. The key here is setting. As with everything else in Germany, there's a time and a place for making jokes. Making a joke at the pub is acceptable while making one in the office usually isn't.

Shopping

4
DON'T SPEND MORE THAN YOU HAVE

While credit cards are popular shopping accessories in most Western countries, Germans pay for just about everything in cash. It doesn't matter whether they're shopping at a small local shop, the supermarket, or a major international store; you'll rarely see a German pay for their purchases with a credit card. With the exception of a few international chains, most places won't accept them (or foreign debit cards) either.

It isn't that Germans don't have credit cards. A lot do. But rather than use them they tend to keep them hidden away in their wallets or sock drawers, only taking them out for emergencies or when travelling. Using a credit card means risking the possibility of getting into debt and Germans are very careful when it comes to anything that might lead to that.

Even the idea of taking out a mortgage and buying a home is a fairly new one in Germany. Renting is extremely common and unlike other countries, it's not seen as a short-term solution either, for example, for students or for someone who hasn't quite got the minimum deposit to buy a property ready yet. In Germany, most people rent late into adult life, and only start to think about a mortgage when they have a very sizeable deposit to put down.

The really cautious even buy their houses outright. Times are changing, and the concept of 'getting on the property ladder' is becoming more of an aspiration, but the pressure to get on it isn't as common as it is in other countries.

There are many theories as to why Germans are so careful with money. Like every other theory about the Germans, they are rooted in 20th-century history.

Psychologists and linguists note that the words for debt (schuld) and guilt (schuld) are the same in German, suggesting that there may be a subconscious connection between the two.

Sociologists take a stab at explaining it by pointing to the reparations Germany was forced to pay after each world war, and the long-term effects hyperinflation would have had on the perception of money.

Another theory highlights the fact that credit cards track spending habits. Germans, who are extremely cautious when it comes to personal privacy, aren't likely to give up this kind of information to any company, especially a financial one.

The problem with all of these theories (and any other theory that people come up with to explain why Germans do the things they do) is that they stem from the last century. Germans have moved on, and it's hard to say how much the past has influenced the current generation's attitudes towards debt.

The reality might be a lot simpler than academics care to admit. Credit card payments are costly for merchants to process and Germans tend to be very rational, even when it comes to shopping. Paying with the money you have in your bank account and not getting into debt just makes a lot more sense.

5
SHOP WITH PREIS-LEISTUNGS-VERHÄLTNIS IN MIND

In Germany, spending decisions are consciously and unconsciously evaluated by a ratio known as Preis-Leistungs-Verhältnis, a ratio of price to quality. If a German is particularly proud of a new purchase, they'll be more likely to highlight the price quality ratio rather than the fact that it came in their favourite colour.

Germans are frugal by nature. Frugal, in this case, doesn't mean buying the cheapest products. In fact, the opposite is often true. Germans typically buy German-made products, products that have a higher price tag but, traditionally at least, are extremely well-made.

But despite being happy to pay more for higher-quality products, Germans are still frugal when it comes to parting with their cash and will spend a lot of time shopping around to get the best value for money. They also tend to spend time researching and comparing the different products available, just to make sure that they really are getting the best deal.

You'll see how companies react and market to this mentality when you shop at a German supermarket. Most supermarkets in Germany are discount supermarkets like Aldi or Lidl, shops that seem to make little or no effort to look nice or make their products look presentable. Instead they focus on the two most important things to the German market, price and quality.

Often when talking about a product, you'll be asked why you chose that particular product over another. Impulse shopping and shopping without research tends to be looked down upon so this is a good opportunity for you to talk about Preis-Leistungs-Verhältnis. Going into a little detail about how you compared all of the different products and found the best possible price is like talking dirty to a German and will earn you their respect for many years to come.

6
TAKE OUT EVERY INSURANCE POLICY AVAILABLE

Germans like to organize and plan their lives meticulously. They can get quite upset if the unexpected happens, especially if it means changing their long term plans.

Unfortunately, life doesn't always turn out as planned. But while the rest of us knock on wood and hope everything will be okay, Germans do their best to plan for the unexpected by taking out insurance policies for every conceivable eventuality.

There's health insurance, which is usually paid into the public health insurance system (Gesetzliche Krankenversicherung) unless you earn over a certain amount in which case it's the private system (Private Krankenversicherung). Then there are all of the standard private insurance policies that you find everywhere else, policies like home, car, and travel insurance. Along with these policies, Germany has a few of its own that tend to be fairly niche in the rest of the world. Three of the most popular are:

Privathaftpflichtversicherung (Personal liability insurance)
Berufsunfähigkeitsversicherung (Disability insurance)
Rechtschutzversicherung (Legal expenses insurance)

Privathaftpflichtversicherung
Imagine you've been invited around to a friend's house for dinner. Then, after a few glasses of wine, you accidentally

knock over their favourite vase. The scene that follows is usually an awkward one where you offer to pay, and they refuse to accept, all the while discreetly moving the bottle of wine out of your reach.

In Germany, you simply swap insurance details. Privathaftpflichtversicherung covers you for all sorts of accidents. It covers you for breaking something in a shop, hitting someone while riding your bike, or injuring someone else while playing sports. It also covers you if your child or dog causes any of these accidents as well.

Mention that you don't have Privathaftpflichtversicherung and most Germans will look at you like you're mad. They'll probably ask you how you can live so recklessly or, "what happens if you break someone else's vase?" Don't be surprised if they get up and run around the room, hiding anything that's remotely breakable.

Berufsunfähigkeitsversicherung
Berufsunfähigkeitsversicherung is a disability insurance policy that covers you if you have an accident and are unable to work. Although disability insurance is available in most countries, it's usually only popular with a small fraction of the population. In Germany roughly a quarter of the population take out this policy.

Losing your job and not having this policy could mean a situation where you'd have to take out a loan or credit card to keep yourself afloat. Germans, as we've already discussed, are very wary of debt. This policy taps into that German need and offers them some psychological security and the ability to 'plan' for the worst.

Now, if only there were insurance policies that covered you in case you didn't find the best Preis-Leistungs-Verhältnis when doing your shopping. Or a policy that covered you in the event that a neighbour saw you crossing the road when there wasn't a green man. That type of cover could definitely go down well in Germany.

Rechtschutzversicherung

Rechtschutzversicherung covers you should you need legal assistance. This policy isn't as popular as personal liability insurance; but along with liability insurance, it might be worth getting it if you're moving to Germany. If you get yourself into any complicated legal messes (for example with a landlord or an employer), your Rechtschutzversicherung should cover the legal costs.

The one area that legal assistance insurance doesn't cover is divorce. It seems insurance companies aren't willing to bank on Germans being particularly easy people to spend a lifetime with. So if you meet the love of your life in Germany, make sure you're positively certain that they're the one before committing to a life of sausages and sauerkraut.

Work

7
BE AS BLUNT AS YOU LIKE

Germans can be very direct to the point of being blunt, particularly in the North of Germany.

A good example of this bluntness can be found in office meetings when someone shares a really bad idea. In most countries, there would be an awkward silence where everyone (including the person who had the bad idea) reflects on just how terrible it was. Eventually someone will break the silence and politely say something along the lines of "that's very nice, but how about..."

In Germany, don't be surprised if you don't hear more than a short and sweet "nein". For Germans, letting someone down gently is seen as an inefficient use of time that could otherwise be spent discussing the good ideas. It sounds blunt, and it is, but from a German point of view it means that everyone knows exactly where they stand, and there's no confusion later on.

Similarly, if you begin the office meeting by talking about the weather, don't expect to engage many people in conversation. Unless the people that you're speaking to are familiar (and accepting) of this weird foreign custom of chit-chat, most won't know how to respond. Say "it's a nice day today" and the person you're speaking to will probably look confused and wonder why you're standing there stating the obvious when you should be talking about what's on the agenda.

Talking about the weather (or specifically, complaining about the weather) is a popular German pastime. But like everything else in Germany, there's a time and a place for it. As a foreigner, it can be hard to know when the appropriate time is, but just understand that it's not during a meeting.

There's a fine line between German bluntness and actual rudeness, and as a newcomer to Germany it can be hard to know which is which. British and Americans tend to struggle most as British people tend to be incredibly polite while America has a culture of being super-friendly and cheerful all of the time; two extremes that don't exist in Germany. Initially you'll just have to give people the benefit of the doubt and chalk any misunderstandings up to cultural differences.

The exception to this is people that work in customer service roles like supermarket cashiers and serving staff in restaurants. If you get the impression that these people are being rude and unfriendly, they probably are. Perhaps it's because Germans don't do chit-chat, but Germany doesn't tend to do customer service very well (or at all). Even Germans find the customer service in Germany unfriendly.

Customer service staff aside, Germans just like to be direct, that's all. Often this comes out as blunt, in the case of the office meeting example, but to a German this is just being honest, and Germans like to be honest all of the time. Even CVs are left unexaggerated.

Although it takes a bit of getting used to, you'll come to appreciate just how efficient this bluntness makes life in Germany. You'll be thankful for the directness in office meetings, especially when you consider that the German working week is shorter than that of most English-speaking countries. You'll also realise that Germans are some of the most genuine people in the world. If someone compliments you on your idea, your handbag, or your new haircut, they genuinely mean it. The downside is that if you try on a pair of jeans and ask a German "does my bum look big in this?" you'll find out just how large your rear end is.

8
BE PUNCTUAL

Punctuality is important in Germany, and it permeates every area of life. Go to a German wedding and you'll see that even the bride turns up on time. As entertaining as the concept of a late bride is for other nations, it's been slow to take off in Germany.

In Germany, if you get invited to a party that starts at 8:00 pm, that usually means be there between approximately 8:00 pm and 8:15 pm. Any earlier or later may be considered rude. Although some Germans are familiar with the concept of arriving 'fashionably late', not every German is, and those that are don't always accept it either. To avoid offending, it's usually best to err on the side of caution, at least until you get to know your host (and the other guests) properly.

Considering that a party is supposed to be a relaxed affair, you can imagine just how important punctuality might be for non-relaxed settings such as the workplace. In 2014, Russian President Vladimir Putin learnt this the hard way when he turned up late for a meeting with Angela Merkel. She did the only reasonable thing any German would do and promptly cancelled the meeting.

Germans are so obsessed with everything happening at the agreed time that in some towns when the clocks switch over to standard time, the trains stop en route for an hour so that they can pull into the station at the correct time.

The only area of life where punctuality is not an obsession is at university. Here, it is acceptable to arrive fifteen minutes after the allotted time, referred to as "Akademisches Viertel", indicated in schedules with a c.t. or cum tempore (Latin for 'with time') beside the start time.

Actually, universities aren't any more laid back than the rest of German society; classes just tend to start fifteen minutes on the dot after they are supposed to. The extra fifteen minutes is to give students and lecturers time to have a break or walk to their respective class. Other countries may accept that students will be late for class, but Germany needed to invent a whole new time system to account for it.

But while all Germans love punctuality, few have taken it to heart quite as much as the renowned philosopher Immanuel Kant. According to popular lore, Kant would get up every morning at exactly 5:00, go to the university at 7:00, and work from 9:00 to 13:00. At exactly 15:30 he would walk up and down the Lindenallee in Königsberg seven times, never more and never less. Rumour has it that some residents of Lindenallee even set their watches by him.

Most Germans aren't quite as predictable or punctual as Kant, although, in a country where punctuality is a virtue that's akin to godliness, it's not hard to imagine a reality where they could be.

9
WORK TIME IS FOR WORK (AND NOTHING ELSE)

The German workplace tends to be a fairly efficient but not particularly fun place to work. The actual level of efficiency versus fun does depend a lot on the industry that you work in, but in comparison to other countries it does seem like a lot more work gets done here. This is maybe because Germans have a shorter working week than most other countries and that doesn't leave much time for chatting around the coffee machine, checking Facebook, or being polite to people when they share a bad idea.

There are pros and cons to German workplace efficiency. A shorter working week means that you will have more free time to yourself, time to pursue a hobby or play a sport for example. However, because you'll have been working so productively, there's a good chance you won't have been able to make friends with anyone at work, and so you'll have to limit yourself to hobbies like stamp collecting and solo sports like long jump.

Workplace meetings, again, offer a great opportunity to see German efficiency in action. While in other countries meetings are often an opportunity to "brainstorm" or to "throw some ideas around", Germans tend to come to meetings with their research already done, and their minds made up. The meeting is more of a forum to debate points that have already been thought out and thoroughly researched (often with reams of graphs and statistics to back that research up).

If you're about to attend your first German meeting, don't try to say something clever, or contribute to the conversation for the sake of doing so, as this will usually backfire. Germans are specialists rather than generalists and will only really be interested in your opinion if you are an expert on that subject. Even then, most people will be quite happy to challenge it, without giving much thought to your feelings. It isn't necessarily that they don't like you, or even disagree with you. The aim of a German meeting is to thoroughly debate every point so that at the end of the meeting everyone leaves with the "right" answer.

Another easy mistake is to clap at the end of a speech. Don't! Germans, for whatever reason, don't clap. Instead, they knock on the table with their knuckles. There's no particular benefit to knocking instead of clapping, and nobody knows why the Germans do it, not even the Germans. But even though there's no particular benefit to doing it, knocking is an important German tradition. It's common in offices and even more so in universities, and getting it wrong is considered a major faux pas. The only time clapping is acceptable is if there's nothing to knock on, but triple check that there isn't, as people will look at you strangely if you clap when you could have knocked.

If it gets to the end of the day and someone starts knocking on the table, you might assume you've done something exceptional. Don't take a bow just yet as you probably haven't. Germans also like to knock on wood when it's time to leave, rather than wave. Usually, this is accompanied by "ich mach mal so" (I will just go like this), and obviously them leaving the room as well, so it should be pretty clear whether you're getting a German round of applause or not.

In fact, the odds are fairly stacked against you getting one. Germans aren't that big on praise and don't see why someone would ever say something like "keep up the good work buddy", essentially congratulating someone for just doing their job. Of course, this means if someone does congratulate you, you're doing really well, and you can look forward to a nice round of table knocking (and maybe even a promotion) in the future.

It may seem like Germans are well-oiled, hard-working machines, but it's important to point out that Germans aren't the same people outside of work that they are inside it. Outside of work these same people can be the life and soul of the party (a German party, anyway) but in the office they'll be formal and stiff, even if you were at the same party doing shots of Schnapps and Jägermeister with them. Germans just tend to keep two personas; one for the workplace and one for outside of it. The best advice, which applies to every aspect of German life, is to follow the "when in Rome" approach and just copy what everyone else does.

10
BRING YOUR OWN CAKE INTO THE OFFICE ON YOUR BIRTHDAY

As you get older, birthdays are anticipated with equal measures of excitement and trepidation. While another birthday means you're yet another year older, there's always that silver lining: there'll be cake. Getting a slice of it might mean enduring a cringe-worthy rendition of happy birthday from everyone in the office but the fact that they remembered your special day is touching. After work, there's usually a few drinks in the pub or a meal out, and since it's your birthday everyone always outright refuses to let you pay (not that you were being that persistent).

That's not how it works in Germany. Here, if you go out for a birthday meal or drinks, it's custom to not only pay your way but everyone else's as well. At the very least you should pay for their drinks. As for the cake, it's your job to bring that into the office.

The same thinking applies on your last day in the office. Once again the responsibility of planning a leaving party falls on you. Cake and coffee is always a winner in Germany, but depending on what the last person did, something more extravagant like finger food and drinks might be expected (beer and Sekt being two favourites).

Although it's hard to leave the office without everyone knowing that you're leaving, it's a little easier (seemingly) to get by without bringing a cake into the office on your birthday. After all, nobody at work has mentioned anything, so they've probably all forgotten when it is anyway.

More than likely they've remembered. In Germany, it's extremely bad luck to wish someone happy birthday before the day itself. For such a practical group of people, the Germans are incredibly superstitious. Exactly what they're worried will happen is unclear, but considering you already have to foot the bill for your own party it's probably best not to find out.

But even though birthdays in Germany mean bringing in your own cake and picking up the tab for everyone else's drinks, you do still get presents. Thankfully you won't be presented with a bill for them either.

On the day itself everyone will also wish you a happy birthday, or more commonly in Germany, congratulations (Herzlichen Glückwunsch zum Geburtstag), presumably for making it this far in life without having to declare bankruptcy.

11
REMEMBER YOUR SIES AND DUS

When you speak to people in German, it's important that you address them correctly, particularly in workplace settings where formality and hierarchy are important. Getting it wrong can easily offend and you'll be told if you've made a faux pas. (As if learning German wasn't hard enough!)

Generally speaking, if you don't know the person you're addressing, and if it's within a business context, you should address them using the polite "Sie" form, especially if they're older than you. Also, rather than calling them by their first name, call them Herr or Frau plus their surname instead e.g. Herr Schmidt or Frau Schmidt. That is unless they have a Ph.D., in which case you should call Herr Schmidt Herr Dr Schmidt. Many Germans take titles like 'doctor' and 'professor' incredibly seriously, and will be offended if you do not address them correctly.

This formality doesn't apply to every workplace. Startups or companies within creative industries, for example, tend to have a considerably less formal working culture and most people will address each other with the "Du" form. It usually doesn't apply when two people under the age of thirty address each other either: in most of these cases the "Du" form is automatically used.

If you aren't fortunate enough to work within a creative industry, you'll have to tread carefully as you work out what's appropriate for each conversation. The best approach is to start off with the "Sie" form and if the person isn't particularly bothered by such formalities, they will tell you that it's okay to use the "Du" form. This means you can also use their first name, rather than address them as Herr or Frau.

Moving from the "Sie" to the "Du" form is a big moment in any relationship, and may even represent the start of a lifelong friendship. Just remember that the person with the higher social standing (usually whoever's older) must give the invitation to use the "Du" form. It's usually not appropriate to ask for that invitation, and it can be quite embarrassing if you get refused.

Where it gets particularly tricky is when you meet people who are older than you, but don't consider themselves old. From their point of view, using the Sie form is essentially pointing out how old they are, something they might be trying to ignore. Even trickier for non-natives is trying to hold a conversation with several people in a group if they're all different ages, and trying to remember which person you use the "Du" form with and which one the "Sie".

In particular, it's important always to address a policeman as "Sie". Using the "Du" form could land you a fine of up to €600.

Socialising & Freizeit

12
HAVE SOMETHING TO DO IN YOUR FREIZEIT

Germans will often talk about their "Freizeit" (free time) or ask you what you do with yours. Although the truth might be lying in bed or getting drunk, what they're asking you is what your hobbies are. Germans like to be productive at all times, including their free time, and struggle with Teutonic guilt if they don't use that time wisely.

Being a member of a choir, tending your allotment (Schrebergarten), and garden gnome collecting are all popular hobbies and acceptable ways to pass your free time. The list is essentially endless, and it doesn't matter so much what your hobby is, but that you take it seriously. For example, if you like hiking, it isn't enough to just go for a walk in the woods now and then, or even every weekend. Ideally, you should join a hiking club as well and even better; take out a subscription to German Walking Weekly.

It may seem nerdy to take such a thorough interest in your hobby, but as a foreigner living in Germany you'll be thankful for this German obsession. As we've already mentioned, it can be difficult to make friends at work as Germans tend to keep their colleagues and friends in two separate categories. However since walking, singing in a choir, and garden gnome collecting all fall outside of work hours, you'll find that people are more open and more willing to consider your potential as a friend. And since you share a common love of garden gnomes or walking trails in the Black Forest, it's often acceptable to use the "Du" form from the get go.

Clubs and societies can also be social affairs, with regular annual get-togethers such as the annual Spargel (asparagus) or Gruenkohl (green cabbage) dinners. These might not sound like the most riveting events to add to your social calendar, but they are events nonetheless, and a good opportunity for you to make friends and get to know people.

13
BE ORGANISED &
PLAN EVERYTHING IN ADVANCE

Germans love to plan. Regardless of whether it's for an upcoming meeting, that trip to Mallorca in two years' time or ways to progress in a hobby, there's nothing that can't benefit from a little planning. The longer in advance you plan, and the more detailed and professional you make that plan, the more likely you are to achieve it. At least, that's the German mentality when it comes to planning.

Travel is a good example of this. It's not uncommon for Germans to book their trip a year or more in advance. After all, it ensures you get the best possible Preis-Leistungs-Verhältnis on flights and accommodation. Book a trip two weeks in advance and eyebrows will be raised, as everyone knows that prices go up the closer to the departure date that you book.

Planning is such a big part of the German psyche that everyone expects everyone else to be organised as well. Invite someone to an event that's within the next few weeks and you'll get strange looks for leaving it so last minute. Run out of petrol on the autobahn and well, that's actually illegal. Running out of fuel because you forgot to fill up is not considered an accident; it's something that you could have avoided had you done a little planning!

All of the planning and organisation means that spontaneity

doesn't really exist in Germany, at least not the rest of the world's definition of it. It's rare, if not completely unheard of, for a group of German friends to meet up without having a plan of what they are going to do that day. While spontaneity to everyone else would be "winging it", German spontaneity would be not knowing exactly what you are going to do, but having a multiple choice selection of possibilities that you've thought out in advance.

If you are organised and love to plan, you'll fit in. You'll also earn the respect, admiration, and maybe even friendship of other people in Germany as well.

14
LOVE FUSSBALL

"Football is a simple game. Twenty-two men chase a ball for 90 minutes and at the end, the Germans always win." – Gary Lineker

For many Germans, football is "die schönste Nebensache der Welt" (the best minor matter in the world). Learn a few stats about the players and clubs in the Bundesliga and you'll never find yourself short of a conversation partner. This is especially true during World Cup years when the entire country comes down with a strong case of World Cup Fever.

Like beer, football is a unisex passion and it isn't just limited to a small group of fanatics either. Watch a match in Germany and you'll find yourself cheering beside men, women, kids, and even grandparents.

Germany has one of the best football teams in the world, and some of the best clubs as well. Perhaps this is because German players take a no-nonsense approach to football and are considerably less flamboyant than their Southern European or Latin counterparts, an approach that is best summed up in the famous German quote "Das Runde muss ins Eckige" (the round thing must go in the rectangular thing). It may not be poetic, but it certainly works for them.

Aside from loving football and taking an interest in the Bundesliga, it's important that you hate FC Bayern Munich. (Unless, of course, you're living in Munich). Bayern is one of the richest states in Germany and FC Bayern Munich is one of the most successful football clubs in Europe. Bayern Munich fans are not known for being particularly modest about all of their successes and so tend to be resented by everyone else in Germany.

Bayern-bashing is a good way to make friends in Germany. Just be sure to check that the person you're speaking to isn't a Bayern fan first.

15
HIDE YOUR IDENTITY ONLINE

From search engines tracking the hundreds of questions we ask them every day, to social media sites having access to all of our likes and dislikes, tech companies are privy to an incredible amount of personal information. This lack of privacy is something that's a concern for all of us, but it's something most of us do relatively little about.

In Germany the issue isn't ignored. Despite Germany's thriving tech industry (Berlin is often referred to as the Silicon Valley of Europe) new technologies are usually treated with a great deal of suspicion, at least until personal privacy issues have been clarified.

In practice, this means that if you make a German friend there's a good chance you won't be able to find them on Facebook or any other social media site. Although it breaks the terms and conditions of a lot of websites, Germans are often unwilling to supply their real name and will instead use a nickname, an abbreviation, or just not join the site at all.

As with most other aspects of German culture, concerns over privacy have their roots in Germany's all too recent past. In living memory, personal privacy has been abused by both the Gestapo and Stasi. Then in 2014 it was also revealed that the NSA had been spying on German officials. With firsthand experience of agencies who know too much, Germans tend to be very cautious about what information they give to companies and new technologies.

16
GO DUTCH WHEN IT'S TIME TO PAY

Go out for a meal in Germany and you'll see that German restaurant culture differs ever so slightly from other parts of the world. Firstly, rather than wait to be seated, it's custom just to find a table and seat yourself.

Then, when it comes to paying the bill, the bill is usually split (known as 'Going Dutch'). While splitting the bill is a concept that's by no means unique to Germany, it's rarely done to the same degree of preciseness in most other countries.

When you ask for the bill, the waiter will ask you whether you want to pay "zusammen oder getrennt" (together or separate). If you choose getrennt, and this is by far the most popular answer in Germany, the waiter will then go around the table, work out exactly what everyone had, and present each person with an individualised bill. (Unfortunately, you don't get the option of paying getrennt when it's your birthday.)

Although you would expect this love of the precise to lead to a similar preciseness when it comes to tipping, tipping isn't as big a deal as it is in North America. In Germany, tips are usually just rounded up, often to just a Euro or two and rarely to more than ten Euros.

After your first experience of Going Dutch, you'll leave the restaurant with mixed feelings. On the one hand, you'll have paid exactly what you owe. You'll have avoided that awkward situation where you've only had a salad while everyone else has had a steak, but you've still split the bill equally. At the same time, you'll miss the days when meals out were more casual and relaxed affairs. Itemised breakdowns are best left for tax audits.

17
KNOW YOUR (GERMAN) CULTURE

Although most Germans are well-versed in English-speaking films, literature, and bands, Germany also has some great cultural contributions of its own that are worth exploring. The following is a quick overview of some of the most important elements of German culture that you should at least be aware of, if not watch, read, and listen to.

TV Shows
Tatort
For more than ten million Germans, Sunday night is Tatort night. Tatort is a weekly crime show that's been running on the German public TV channel ARD since 1970, and it's a big part of the collective consciousness. Every Sunday a team of investigators from a different region or city in Germany solve a tough case, usually a murder case.

There are 21 different versions of Tatort, each produced by the regional branches of ARD. There's a Tatort based in every major German city. There's even a Tatort based in Vienna, and a Tatort based in Lucerne. Each region contributes a couple of episodes each year, so every week there's a different set of detectives and a new area of Germany on display. One week you might be watching two hardened Berlin detectives solve a murder in Kreuzberg, and the next week it could be two country cops solving an environmental case in Konstanz.

Occasional Tatort watchers are rare in Germany, and those

that watch Tatort do so religiously. Many will go to Tatort nights at local bars and restaurants or have friends over to watch it and bet on the culprit. Everyone has their favourite Tatort team (usually the local one), and it is discussed almost as much as football. Even abroad, wherever there are large communities of German expats or holidaymakers, you'll find Tatort nights happening.

Tatort isn't exactly Hollywood or even CSI. As a non-German you probably won't get what the fuss is about, at least initially. Don't try to understand the obsession, just smile and embrace it instead. Because Tatort is set in a new city or region every week, it's a good opportunity to learn about different regional German customs, dialects, mentality, and architecture.

German Telenovelas
As with almost all soaps, Germans soaps tend to be poor-quality with a strong focus on dramatic storytelling. Popular German soaps include Unter Uns, Sturm der Liebe, Verbotene Liebe, and the very popular Gute Zeiten, Schlechte Zeiten.

Lindenstraße (1985 - today)
Based on the British soap, Coronation Street, Lindenstraße has been running for more than thirty years. It follows the lives of several key characters living on Lindenstraße, a fictional street in Munich.

Stromberg (2004 - today)
Stromberg is the German adaptation of the British and American comedy show 'The Office'. Besides being funny, Stromberg is a good opportunity to see some of the clichés of German office life portrayed on screen.

Der Tartortreiniger (2011 - today)
A comedy show about a crime scene cleaner, Der Tartortreiniger is more of a comedy show than a crime one, particularly slapstick comedy. With subtitles, Der

Tartortreiniger is one of the easiest German comedy shows for non-natives to watch.

Deutschland 83 (2015)
Deutschland 83 is a new TV show that follows a 24-year-old East German spy who gets sent to West Germany to work undercover for the Stasi. Set in 1983, the year of the Nato-Double-Track-Decision, this TV series gives a good idea of what daily life was like on both sides of the wall.

Movies
Lola Rennt (Run Lola Run, 1998)
An arty 90s film in which Lola has to obtain 100,000 Deutsche Mark in just 20 minutes to save her boyfriend's life.

Das Leben Der Anderen (The Lives of Others, 2006)
A film about a Stasi officer (Gerd Wiesler) who starts spying on an East German playwright and his actress lover, both of whom he believes are disloyal to the state. Although the film starts out with Wiesler looking for a way to catch the couple out, spying on them means he gets to know the couple intimately, and over the course of the film becomes surprisingly sympathetic to them.

Goodbye Lenin (2003)
In October 1989, right before the fall of the Berlin Wall, Alex Kerner's mum falls into a coma. When she comes out, he and his sister Ariane, must work hard to pretend that communism is still in force for fear that the truth will give her a heart attack.

Der Baader Meinhof Komplex (The Baader Meinhof Complex, 2008)
The Red Army Faction (RAF), a group of left-wing extremists, embark on a campaign of violence, bombings, robberies, kidnappings, and assassinations against the German state.

Das Boot (1981)
An intense war epic that takes you onboard U-96, a German

WWII submarine, and shows you the horrors of war from deep under the water.

Der Untergang (Downfall, 2004)
Set in his Berlin bunker, Der Untergang shows the last ten days of Adolf Hitler's life as he and his fellow Nazi leaders come to realise that the end is in sight for all of them.

Die Welle (The Wave, 2008)
Loosely based on a psychological experiment known as "The Third Wave", the film tells the story of a German teacher who tries to show his students how a dictatorship could happen in a modern Germany. As the students begin to accept the idea, things quickly start to spin out of control.

Victoria (2015)
Filmed in one single shot, this story takes place over the course of one night. It follows Victoria, a girl from Spain, on a night out in Berlin. What begins as a typical night out quickly escalates once she meets locals Sonne, Boxer, Blinker, and Fuß, and finds herself trapped in a hopeless situation that seems to offer no escape.

Berlin Calling (2008)
A tragicomedy that takes you on a journey into Berlin's early electro and techno scene as it looks at the events that lead to DJ and producer Ickarus's (Paul Kalkbrenner) institutionalization for drug abuse.

Literature
For non-natives, even those with an excellent grasp of German, German literature can be hard to read as German authors tend to use complex language, sometimes seemingly for the sake of complexity itself. That said, it's worth persevering as Germany has some great authors. In particular, four modern German authors have received the Nobel Prize for literature: Thomas Mann (The Magic Mountain), Hermann

Hesse (Siddhartha), Heinrich Böll (The Clown), and Günter Grass (The Tin Drum).

Poetry

Goethe is probably the most admired German poet, but other well-known German poets to explore include Lessing, Schiller, Kleist, Hoffmann, Brecht, and Schmidt. Don't worry if you struggle to read them, so do a lot of Germans. German poetry is even harder to read than German literature making it particularly unpopular with high school students who have to read the classics in school. Some of the most well-known poems are Goethe's "Die Leiden des jungen Werther" (The sorrows of the young Werther), Iphigenie auf Taurus (Iphigenia in Tauris), Schiller's "Die Räuber", and Lessing's Nathan der Weise (Nathan the Wise).

Philosophy

The stereotype of Germans is that they're rigid and robotic, but in reality they can be incredibly philosophical in their thinking, and will often steer conversations in a philosophical direction. In fact, Germany is often referred to as Das Land der Dichter und Denker (the land of poets and thinkers).

Germany has had a major influence on philosophy and critical thinking, starting with philosophers like Magnus and later Leibniz, right up until more internationally-recognised names like Karl Marx, Immanuel Kant, Georg Wilhelm Friedrich Hegel, Theodor W. Adorno, and Friedrich Wilhelm Nietzsche.

Music

Mention German bands and most people will say Rammstein or Tokio Hotel. While both of these bands are popular in Germany, they're probably more popular outside of Germany than in it. As popular as they are, they're just one of many bands and genres listened to here.

Starting with classical, Germany has produced some of the

most famous musicians in the world. Beethoven, Bach, Brahms, Strauss, and Wagner are just some of the major names to come from Germany, along with Händel, Telemann, Schumann, and Orff.

Aside from a brief musical period in the 20s dominated by Marlene Dietrich and the German "Comedian Harmonists", the German music scene went quiet for a little while. It kicked off again during the Neue Deutsche Welle period at the beginning of the 80s when artists like Nena (99 Luftballons) and Peter Schilling (Major Tom) came onto the scene. These were followed by bands like The Scorpions and Rammstein, both of which are well known internationally, as well as others that aren't as well known like Peter Fox, BAP, Die Toten Hosen, Paul Kalkbrenner, Die Ärzte, Marteria, Deichkind, Xavier Naidoo, and Helene Fischer.

More recently (or since the 90s at least), Germany has been at the forefront of the house and electronic music trend producing famous DJs like Kraftwerk, both Paul & Fritz Kalkbrenner, Paul von Dyk, Sven Väth, Moguai, Boys Noize, Solomun, Tube & Berger, Oliver Koletzki, David August, and many more.

18
DON'T MENTION DAVID HASSELHOFF

While we're on the subject of music, it's probably worth mentioning David Hasselhoff, and whether Germans love him or not. The background to this story is that on New Year's Eve 1989, David Hasselhoff took to the stage at Berlin's iconic Brandenburg Gate and performed the song, "I've Been Looking for Freedom". This particular New Year's Eve was a big event in Germany as the Berlin Wall had come down just over a month before. The fall of the wall put an end to the thirty-year long division between East and West Germany and effectively ended the Cold War.

Naturally, everyone was in high spirits; the happiest they'd been in almost half a century. Many were ringing in the New Year with family and friends that they hadn't seen for decades. When the star of Knight Rider came onstage, the crowd went completely wild. Unfortunately for Germany, someone was there with a video camera. A clip of Germany's guilty pleasure made it all the way to SNL's Weekend Update, a popular US sketch show. They put two and two together and came to the only possible conclusion: Germans love David Hasselhoff.

Once again, Germany's international reputation was tarnished. If that wasn't bad enough, the idea grew into something bigger: that the lyrics of Hasselhoff's hit had somehow caused the German people to search within themselves and look for freedom. Basically, some people started to believe that David Hasselhoff had single-handedly brought down the Berlin Wall and put an end to the madness that was the Cold War.

Things got a little out of hand and Germany has had a slightly awkward relationship with Hasselhoff ever since. There's no denying the love affair of 1989, but the idea that modern German history was shaped by the star of a TV show about a talking car is just a little too much for most Germans to take.

Mentioning David Hasselhoff falls into the same category as talking about the Nazi period. It's something Germany is deeply embarrassed about and they would like it very much if everyone else didn't mention it ever again.

At Home

19
SIT DOWN WHEN YOU PEE

From an early age, German boys are taught to be a Sitzpinkler (someone who sits down to pee) and not a Stehpinkler (someone who stands up to pee). Whether men continue to do so when they get older is another question, but based on the signs in offices, restaurants, and cafes, there's certainly a large enough Sitzpinkler movement to make sure that the rule is upheld.

Along with these signs, some homes have an S.P.U.K. or WC-Geist, a gadget that issues you with a verbal reprimand if it catches you breaking the rules and peeing standing up. These gadgets are available in many different authoritative yet hilarious (to the Germans at least) voices such as former German chancellors Helmut Kohl and Gerhard Schröder.

It isn't just Germany that's passionate about the Sitzpinkler rule. In Sweden, the Left Party is pushing to make standing up while peeing illegal, while in Japan a 2007 poll found that 49% of men sit down when they pee, a major increase from a previous 1999 poll where the figure was only at 15%.

In terms of cleanliness, sitting down to pee is undeniably more efficient. Most men have terrible aim and considering that Germany is one of the biggest alcohol-consuming nations in the world, you can only expect that the same is true in Germany as well.

Sitting down to pee also makes a lot of sense when you consider the design of some German toilets, in particular, the ones with the famous 'inspection shelf'. Standing up at one of these can result in a lot of splashback, forcing even the most determined of Stehpinklers to change his personal views on the issue.

20
DON'T MAKE NOISE ON A SUNDAY

Sunday is a day of rest according to the Christian religion and according to German law as well. You can forget about that lazy Sunday stroll around Ikea, or even doing your weekly grocery shopping. Supermarkets and shops are closed on Sundays, something that can catch a lot of tourists out, and many spend their first Sunday in Germany feeling very hungry.

Although the concept has its roots in religion, even the most atheistic of Germans still respect the idea that Sunday is for relaxing and not making any noise. Hoovering, DIY, recycling last night's bottles, children playing together, and anything else that makes noise should be kept for the other six days of the week. Well, apart from between the hours of 13:00 and 15:00 (Mittagsruhe), traditionally another period of quiet time in Germany, although some regions have now done away with this rule.

Along with quiet Sundays and quiet afternoons, most apartment blocks will also have communal rules that mention noise. There's usually a ban against noise after 21:00, for example using the washing machine. Strangely, there's also a law forbidding tuning pianos at midnight, which given the other rule about noise after 21:00 seems a little unnecessary. Germans are thorough; it has to be said.

Instead of shopping or mowing their lawns, Germans spend Sundays cycling, eating cake and drinking coffee, reading, practicing their hobbies, watching football or the TV, and spending time with family and friends. If you find yourself bored, it's probably because you haven't found a hobby to practice in your Freizeit yet.

The goal of all of these rules and laws is to provide a clear separation between work time and home time. In a world where modern working life can mean working evenings and weekends, the thinking behind these rules is definitely a positive, even if it takes a bit of getting used to.

Along with a shorter working week and relaxing Sundays, Germans also get a very reasonable number of paid days off every year, at least 20 days, not including the 9-13 days of public holidays each region gets as well. While this may not be much to many Europeans, Germans do have the unique benefit of being able to claim up to 5 paid educational days off each year to attend seminars or training events.

Yet, despite all of these work-life balance rules, many Germans struggle to relax and enjoy life, at least according to market research firm Rheingold. It found that 46 percent of Germans felt that they were unable to enjoy anything due to the stress of everyday life and the feeling of being constantly reachable.

Even though shops are closed on Sundays, places to eat such as restaurants, cafés, and bars are usually open, along with takeaways and motorway service stations. The big supermarkets are always closed, but small supermarkets inside train stations are often open.

But instead of trying to find shops that are open, why not embrace this German tradition and keep Sunday as a day of rest? Who knows, it may even be the secret to why Germans are so productive the rest of the week.

21
OWN A SCHREBERGARTEN

Visiting Germany for the first time, a South African remarked, "your townships are really neat!" From a distance, Schrebegartens may look like well-ordered shanty towns but in reality there's nothing shanty about them.

Schrebergärten (also known as Kleingärten) are allotments or plots of land normally found on the outskirts of the city where city residents can grow fruit and vegetables. The concept was the brainchild of Dr. Moritz Schreber, a fairly eccentric 19th-century German physician from Leipzig.

Obsessed with masturbation, which he felt was an incredibly bad way to spend your Freizeit, Schreber spent most of his life inventing mechanical devices to keep teenagers' hands busy. Although Schreber went on to invent the German allotment system, which is a wonderful way for everyone to get their hands dirty without ever touching their genitals, sadly for Schreber he died before he had a chance to see the idea take off.

The Schrebergarten concept means that everyone in Germany, regardless of wealth, can have access to fresh fruit and vegetables. This thinking is a great example of Soziale Marktwirtschaft (social market economy), Germany's ability to have a free market economy without neglecting its societal responsibilities. During the First and Second World War, when cities were all but cut off from the surrounding countryside, the Schrebergarten became more than just a clever left-wing idea and meant that residents of German cities had access to fresh fruit and vegetables at a time when this would have been otherwise impossible.

In 1983, Germany passed the Bundeskleingartengesetz (Federal Small Garden Law), a series of regulations and rules for owning a Schrebergarten. In addition to the Bundeskleingartengesetz - which at nine pages long should be enough regulations for anyone - each colony, or group of Schrebergartens, has a formal leadership that come up with rules on everything Schrebergarten-related. From when you're allowed to mow your lawn, to what colour your garden shed can be, there are rules for just about every aspect of Schrebergarten life.

22
RECYCLE, RECYCLE, RECYCLE

One of the major rules of being German is that you must recycle. If you're spotted emptying your waste without taking the appropriate recycling measures, you can expect anything from a light lecture to a public chastising. It doesn't matter which form of scolding you get, both are equally terrifying when said in German.

As someone living in or visiting Germany, you should try to recycle everything. Every apartment block will have a collection of different coloured bins for all of the various household wastes. There's a bin for plastic wrappers and containers, another for glass, and another for paper and cardboard. There's often a bin for organic waste as well, and in some parks you will see special bins for used barbecue coals.

These bins are the basic ones that cover the majority of household waste. There are also bins where you can recycle batteries, old clothes, unwanted appliances, old furniture, and large household objects. There's even a special day when you can leave your Christmas tree out for recycling (Abholung der Weihnachtsbäume).

Bottles and cans have a slightly different recycling system. Every time you purchase either, you pay a Pfand, a small deposit that you get back when you bring it to a recycling station or newsagents.

If you don't recycle them, someone else will: homeless people regularly scour the street and pick up any cans or bottles they find in exchange for the Pfand.

If you don't understand any aspect of the system, just ask. Most Germans will be more than happy to explain it all to you, although they might wonder what waste-ridden planet you've fallen from. Alternatively, the local council can provide you with a leaflet explaining how it all works.

When recycling started to become important, many EU countries tried to come up with clever ways to coax their citizens into recycling. Germany didn't need to. Recycling combines two of the major aspects of the German psyche: a love of the environment, and the innate desire to be organised. Sorting rubbish into different coloured containers to save the planet is basically heaven for the Germans.

So when in Germany, recycle. Except on Sundays when the rule of being quiet overrides the recycling rule.

23

TAKE YOUR KITCHEN WITH YOU
WHEN YOU MOVE

Germans, and especially Bavarians, like to take everything with
them when they move to a new home. Everything, in this case,
doesn't just mean appliances like the dishwasher and the fridge
but also fitted cupboards, light fixtures, and yes, even the
kitchen sink.

To the outsider, this isn't a particularly efficient way of moving
house, although a German would argue that it's an efficient
way of ensuring you always get the kitchen that you want.
Considering that dishwashers and gas ovens often have the
additional cost of a handyman to fit them, the outsider has a
strong argument here.

When buying or renting in Germany, it's wise to check what
fixtures, furniture, and appliances will be in the house when
you move in, especially if you're renting. Don't make the
assumption that everything in the house belongs to the
landlord and will be there when you move in.

These days more and more rentals come equipped with sinks
and cupboards. If your house doesn't, there's a good chance
that you'll have to buy all of these things yourself. Naturally,
once you've done that you'll also be keen to rip them out of the
wall and take them with you when you go to move as well.

Occasionally you'll get lucky, and the previous tenant will try and sell you their fridge or sink. This sometimes happens if they're moving into a house that already has fitted furniture, or if they're planning on doing a little remodelling once they move in.

Getting Around

24
CYCLE EVERYWHERE
(AND GET ANGRY WHEN YOU CAN'T)

Germans are rational, grounded, law-abiding individuals. Except, that is, when it comes to cycling. There's something about cycling, or more importantly not being able to cycle along a cycle path, that forces those rule-conscious Germans to completely lose their cool. If you see an obstruction in the cycle path, have a look around and you'll probably see a cyclist pedalling up the pavement, teeth gritted, ringing the bike bell in a passionate rage.

To understand why mild-mannered Germans turn into the Hulk if they see an obstructed bike lane, it's essential to understand why cycling is so important in Germany. For most Germans cycling isn't just about getting from A to B. There's an ideological element to it as well. Cycling is about not driving a car, and doing your bit to save the environment. It can also cut down on healthcare costs: adding a work-out to your commute is the ultimate in German efficiency.

Given that health and the environment are important to so many Germans, and cycling is such an obvious way to cut down on your carbon footprint and waistline, German cyclists expect there to be good cycle paths everywhere. They also expect those cycle paths to be clean and well-maintained.

Germany has some of the best infrastructure for cyclists in Europe. In some places, however, there are no cycle paths on smaller roads or sometimes there is a cycle path but road works are being carried out next to it, spilling over and causing an obstruction. This infuriates German cyclists. But instead of getting off their bikes and calmly walking around the mess, or carefully joining the traffic, they'll pedal furiously down the pavement shouting at any pedestrian foolhardy enough to get in their way. Sometimes they'll zip in and out of traffic in an almost suicidal manner, ignoring the screeching of brakes and muttering angrily to themselves.

The only thing that angers a German cyclist more than roadworks and poor infrastructure is people walking in the cycle lane. When tourists and other newcomers inadvertently wander into their path, cyclists see red. The thing is it's easy to step onto the path if you're not used to the system as cycle paths in German cities are usually part of the pavement, not the road. Just a small painted line separates the cycle path from the pedestrian walkway. So, if you don't want to incur the wrath of a bell-ringing German maniac, always look down!

Many newcomers to Germany find it annoying having to spend their lives dodging angry cyclists. After a few months, however, you will quickly realise that you can't beat them, and it makes much more sense just to get a bike and join them.

25
LOVE YOUR CAR

Germans have a special place in their hearts for their cars, especially if it's a German-made car like a BMW, Mercedes, Audi, or Porsche. It isn't that Germans are particularly patriotic, but rather that German cars are well-made and tend to fare well under Preis-Leistungs-Verhältnis scrutiny.

Being a German car lover means spending a lot of your free time cleaning it, polishing it, and talking with pride about its fuel efficiency or horsepower. Some Germans even create Facebook and Twitter profiles for their cars, checking them into places and uploading pictures of their car's adventures.

A good quality car is essential for driving on the German motorways (Autobahn), most of which don't have speed limits. There are exceptions to this of course: some parts have speed limits during poor weather conditions such as snow or rain, but for the most part, you are free to drive as fast as you like. The only real rule, regardless of whether you're driving on a section of the motorway with a speed limit or not, is that you keep your cool. Road rage is illegal in Germany and giving someone the finger could result in a nasty fine.

Autobahns with no speed limits are a controversial topic in Germany, and it's something that's continuously under debate. But although many groups have raised the notion of getting rid of them, none of their petitions or motions have ever gained the support needed.

Even though there are no speed limits on a lot of the autobahns, the majority of people drive fairly sensibly. They usually drive somewhere around 130 kmph (the speed limit of other European motorways). Sure, there are some speed demons that are desperate to see just how fast their German cars can go, but they're definitely a minority.

The Hierarchy of a German Family

26
COMPLAIN ABOUT THE TRAINS

Germans like a good moan. Whether it's about the weather, politicians, celebrities who think too highly of themselves, or football, everything gets moaned about in Germany.

One thing that Germans love to complain about, above pretty much every other gripe, is the trains. Train travel in Germany is neither punctual nor efficient, something that along with the high levels of bureaucracy and the shops closing on Sundays, surprises the millions of foreigners that visit or move to Germany every year.

Of course, an inefficient train system isn't something that's unique to Germany; it's a fact of life in most countries. But as common a problem as it is worldwide, Germans refuse to accept that it should happen in Germany.

Even when the trains do arrive on time, Germans won't be forgiving and will take to complaining about their second biggest Deutsche Bahn complaint: the onboard announcements. Next time you're on a German train, take a moment to listen to the announcement as you arrive at a station.

"Thank you for travelling with Deutsche Bahn".

The problem for Germans is that the accent is so ridiculously German it's almost a parody. Look around when you hear it and it's almost certain that you'll see one or two people shaking their heads.

"Zänk ju for trävelling wis Deutsche Bahn".

The upside to an inefficient train system and an entire country that constantly moans about it is that if you're running late for anything in Germany, anything at all, you can simply blame the trains. Rather than get the usual stern look for being late, people will actually sympathise.

Outlook

27

HARBOUR CONFLICTED FEELINGS OF NATIONAL PRIDE

Germans have a lot to be proud of. Germany is one of the most progressive countries in the world, and its citizens enjoy a great quality of life. It's even more impressive when you realise that the country had to be completely rebuilt from scratch, both physically and morally, while at the same time paying billions in war reparations. Then there's everything that Germany is good at: football, beer, recycling... the list can become fairly lengthy.

But you'll never catch a German saying that they're proud to be German. Displays of national pride like those that you see in the USA, Ireland, or France are unheard of here. Germans, despite having a lot to be proud of, never think to themselves: "you know what? It's great to be German!" At least if they do, they never say it out loud. From the German point of view you didn't choose your nationality. Therefore, you can't be proud of it.

It's only in recent World Cup years that showing a little pride for the German football team has become acceptable. Before 2006, it was rare to see a German flag hanging from anyone's balcony, and even then popular opinion was very divided as to whether that was okay or not. During more recent tournaments, the pride has been more obvious. As well as car flags and novelty wigs, the German flag has been painted onto fingernails, special packs of sweets, and bafflingly onto the eggs in the supermarket as well.

In Germany national pride is a potentially lethal weapon, something that has not only been taken too far in the past, and in the case of Neo-Nazism, is still a problem today. Along with the government making certain things illegal for example: Holocaust denial, Nazi salutes, or displaying the swastika - the German people put a lot of effort into trying to quench extremist displays of national pride.

In 2014, Neo-Nazis announced that they would be making their annual march through Wunsiedel in Bavaria. Wunsiedel is the final resting place of Rudolf Heß, one of the most prominent Nazi leaders.
Neo-Nazis feel about Wunsiedel the way Catholics feel about Lourdes and Muslims feel about Mecca, and in an attempt to prevent Wunsiedel from becoming any more of a far right travel destination, the Center for Democratic Culture came up with a cunning plan. For every metre that the extremists walked, they (and all of the sponsors involved) would donate €10 to EXIT Deutschland, a charity that helps Neo-Nazis and extremists leave the scene. To truly send the message home, they also stood at the side of the road holding bright pink banners that encouraged them to keep walking and keep raising money for EXIT Deutschland.

This isn't the first time that Germans have tried to screw with Neo-Nazis, or even that Wunsiedel has tried to counteract its problem. In 2011 when the 20-year lease on Heß's grave was up for renewal (we told you that Germans like to rent rather than buy), the town and family members agreed to dig him up and bury him at sea instead.

Unfortunately, it didn't stop Neo-Nazis from showing up, and since then the town has been coming up with more creative ways to convince the Neo-Nazis to find somewhere else for their annual pilgrimage.

With extremes like this still such a big problem in Germany, Germans tend to tread very carefully when it comes to displays of national pride. Singing the national anthem is rare, and it's even rarer to see anyone put their hand over their heart if they do sing it.

Although Germans are divided about whether it's acceptable to get patriotic during sports events, nobody raises concerns about it happening during Eurovision. Here, it's perfectly acceptable to wave the German flag and show a little German pride as it's pretty unlikely that doing so will lead to the start of any wars, or incite feelings of national pride in the Neo-Nazi community.

But although you don't see a lot of national pride in Germany, you will see displays of local pride. Germany, at least the Germany we know of today, was founded in 1871. Before that, the country was made up of a patchwork of minor territories, and a few major ones like Prussia and Bavaria. Since 1871 Germany has been through a lot, not least being carved up and divided into two separate countries. It's hardly surprising then that regional pride is as strong as national pride, if not stronger.

To show their pride, Germans often buy locally-produced goods, display local flags as opposed to the national flag, and sing local anthems as well. Since most Germans don't feel comfortable showing any signs of patriotism, local pride is the perfect alternative.

28
LOVE THE GERMAN LANGUAGE

"In early times some sufferer had to sit up with a toothache, and he put in the time inventing the German language."

~ Mark Twain

Mark Twain isn't the only person who's spoken cruelly about the German language. To the rest of the world, German can come across as harsh and aggressive but to most Germans, it's one of the most beautiful languages in the world. And, despite all of Mark Twain's complaining, he continued to learn German for most of his adult life. To the non-native, German will never be as easy on the ear as languages like French and Italian but German has its qualities, and over time most language learners come to appreciate German for what it is.

One of the most enjoyable things about the German language is its preciseness. German words often explain exactly what the item is. The word Handschuh, for example, is exactly that, a shoe (Schuh) for your hand, or a glove. Schweinefleisch (swine flesh) is pork. Brustwarzen are breast warts or nipples while a slug is a Nacktschnecke, or naked snail. But of all the German words, there's no word that's more precise than the German word for the birth control pill: Antibabypille (anti baby pill).

The preciseness of the German language often makes it easy to understand what's being said, even with a limited vocabulary, simply by separating some of the words. The only downside to this is that there's no limit to how many words can be amalgamated into a single new word. Up until recently, the Germans had a word for the law which governed beef label monitoring. This word, Rindfleischetikettierungsüberwach-ungsaufgabenübertragungsgesetz was 63 letters long. It wasn't until the EU changed the cattle testing laws, and the word was no longer relevant, that anyone even considered getting rid of it.

Not all big German words are as long as the one above. Although there are plenty of ridiculously long words, most aren't used in everyday conversation and usually refer to something obscure like beef labelling or the 'widow of a Danube steamboat company captain' (Donaudampf-schifffahrtsgesellschaftskapitänswitwe).

Where the German language really excels though, is with words for which there's no English equivalent. Many of them, like Doppelgänger, Schadenfreude, and Zeitgeist, are so useful that they eventually appear in the English language, but there are plenty that haven't made it in yet.

Treppenwitz (staircase joke) is one example. It describes that moment after a conversation has ended when you think of what would have been the perfect thing to say. Kummerspeck (grief bacon) is the weight you gain through emotional overeating. Drachenfutter (dragon food) is a gift you give your significant other after messing up. Ohrwurm (ear worm) describes a song that gets stuck in your head and follows you around for the rest of the day while Torschlusspanik (closing gate panic) is the feeling that life's opportunities are slipping away.

But even though the German language can be incredibly exact at times, at others it can be incredibly lazy. There are a huge number of words that end with the word zeug (German for 'stuff' or 'thing'). For example, Flugzeug, the German for aeroplane, literally means flying thing. Then there's Feuerzeug or fire thing, which is the German for a lighter and Butterzeug, meaning butter thing, a popular type of buttery German biscuit. More recently, there's been a tendency to introduce new English words without coming up with a German equivalent. Words like blogger, comedian, and logo simply become der Blogger, der Comedian, and das Logo while verbs like to flirt, or outsource become flirten and outsourcen.

While many Germans can speak English, often just as well if not better than some native speakers, it's a good idea to learn a little bit of the lingo if you're planning on staying in Germany. German is difficult for foreigners, but you should give it a try. You'll make mistakes, yes, and you will be corrected, definitely. But don't worry, that's just the German way. Some Germans will even correct your English as well!

There's no doubt that you can get by without knowing German, but not knowing any of the language means missing out on conversations and experiences that you might otherwise get to be a part of if you spoke even a little German. Learning German will also help you settle in better. Germans are very appreciative when foreigners take an interest in their language and culture, although they're often surprised about the latter.

If you leave Germany and return to speaking English, you'll find that you miss certain words that have no English equivalent, words like "Ach so" or "Doch doch". Even swearwords like "Scheiße" sound better in German. Then there are all of the German words that make you giggle on a daily basis, words like Kunst and Ausfahrt.

Of course the biggest argument for learning German is that without it, you'll never have any chance of ever being able to experience the enigma that is the German sense of humour.

29
LOOK DOWN ON THE OSSI / WESSI

Although East and West Germany reunited in 1990, the Berlin wall still stands inside the heads of many Germans.

Western Germans (Wessi) are possibly most guilty of this, resenting the fact that they have to subsidise former Eastern German citizens (Ossi). Re-unifying Germany was expensive and resulted in high unemployment and poverty, particularly in the former East Germany. The German government countered the costs of assisting the poor former East by introducing the solidarity tax (soli), a tax all German citizens have to pay, even to this day.

Ossis aren't without blame either. They resent being looked down on by the 'arrogant' Wessis and in turn look down on the Wessis for being so rude.

Perhaps it's this defensiveness that has kindled the feeling of Ostalgie (nostalgia for East Germany). Although less than 15% of former East Germans would be happy with a return to communism, many Ossis still look back fondly at Trabant cars, state-approved TV shows and the Spreewald gherkins that were a big part of life in the DDR.

Will the differences between the Ossi and Wessi ever disappear? Stereotypes are hard to shift and some remnants of these attitudes might always exist. Then again, there are adults today who weren't even born when the wall came down. It's possible that, over the next generation or two, these attitudes will disappear, especially as former East German cities like Berlin, Leipzig, and Dresden continue to become some of the most popular places to live for Ossi, Wessi, and foreigners alike.

30
DON'T MAKE NAZI JOKES

Nazi jokes in English-speaking countries go back a long way. In cinema culture films like Charlie Chaplin's The Great Dictator (1940) and Mel Brooks's The Producers (1968) both have plenty of giggles at the expense of the Third Reich. To most Germans, however, the Nazi period is no laughing matter, so regardless of how funny you think your joke is, it's probably best left unsaid.

Aside from being insensitive, one of the main reasons Nazi jokes don't go over well in Germany is that the subject just isn't seen as a humorous one. From a young age, Germans visit concentration camps and war memorials to learn firsthand about the atrocities and to reflect on what happened. In times gone by, Holocaust survivors would also visit schools to speak about their terrible experiences.

Reminders of what's obviously a very embarrassing and distressing past don't stop when you leave school either. As adults, Germans are constantly reminded about the Nazi period through the war monuments that dot almost every corner of every German city, to the endless series of Nazi and WWII documentaries shown on German television, particularly N24. The focus is always Vergangenheitsbewältigung (coming to terms with the past) and dealing with Kollektivschuld (inherited collective guilt).

Consequently, blasé mentions of Nazis like "he was a total

Nazi about it" will be seen as inconsiderate while doing a Nazi salute is definitely not funny, particularly if you're the person doing it. Nazi salutes are illegal in Germany and doing one could see you spending time in jail or facing a hefty fine. Likewise, if you call an official a Nazi, or a "Little Hitler," you could be fined up to €5000. Some German government department seems to have kept track of all the different swearwords and has come up with appropriate fines depending on the severity of the word. Call someone a Schweinehund and that'll cost you €10 while calling someone an Arschloch (asshole) will cost you €20. Call someone a Hurensohn (son of a whore), and, well you might need to take out a loan to pay for that.

There have been some German attempts to make light of the situation. Obersalzberg, a TV show with a cult following, parodies Stromberg (the German equivalent of The Office) and follows the lives of an inefficient Hitler and his equally inefficient crew working in a modern office setting. Then there's Front Deutscher Äpfel (The German Apple front), a satirical political organisation that makes fun of Neo-Nazis and their pure race values. Front Deutscher Äpfel's demands include closing the border to all non-German fruits in an attempt to highlight how ridiculous Neo-Nazi beliefs are.

British people often say, "don't mention the war," and assume that Germans must have blocked that part of history out of their heads. In reality, the opposite is true. The Nazi period gets talked about a lot, just rarely in a comical way.

A better piece of advice would be: don't joke about the war. In Germany, it's almost never considered a funny topic. So, if you want to break the ice with a group of Germans, leave your best Hitler jokes at home.

31

SUFFER FROM AN EVER-INCREASING LIST OF HEALTH PROBLEMS

Many Germans take their health very seriously. This isn't surprising when you realise just how many unusual illnesses Germans can come down with, most of which seem to be unheard of outside of Germany. If your colleague has had to take the day off work, there's a good chance he's suffering from one of these German ailments:

Kreislaufprobleme (circulatory collapse) - As common illnesses go, this sounds incredibly worrying, but it's something Germans will very matter-of-factly tell you they have. Even though it sounds life-threatening, most people recover in a day or two.

Föhnkrankheit - This is common in Bavaria and most mountainous regions of Germany. Föhn is the name for a very specific wind, a wind that cools the air as it goes up one side of the mountain, and then warms and compresses it as it comes down the other. It may seem incredibly technical, but in Bavaria and other mountainous regions of Germany everyone understands it, and it's the case of many a sick day.

Frühjahrsmüdigkeit (early year tiredness) - While many of us feel tired at the start of the year, in Germany it's considered an illness and something that can put you in bed for a couple of days.

Hörsturz (sudden loss of hearing) - This is the most dramatic of all the German maladies, but move to Germany and you'll meet people who have either suffered from this ailment or know people that have.

You might be thinking that Germans sound like a bunch of neurotics. Not everyone succumbs to these illnesses, but Germany definitely has a fair share of people who get overly hung up on their health. There's even a special weather report known as Biowetter that attempts to predict the illnesses that you can expect to come down with. It's essentially a horoscope for hypochondriacs, and it's usually accurate, although the reasons are probably more due to psychosomaticism than anything else.

Fear of getting ill has lead to an unusual relationship with the air, which Germans both fear and revere at the same time. On the one hand, Germans are terrified of any kind of draught or cold air, and try to keep the windows shut at all times. Make the mistake of opening the window on a train and you'll hear shouts of "es zieht" while people jump out of their seats and run down the aisle to close it. At the same time, however, there are just as many concerns about not changing the air regularly; putting everyone in a catch-22 situation where they have to decide which one is currently more concerning.

Air concerns aren't just a winter phenomenon either. Even in the middle of summer you'll see people wearing scarves to protect themselves from the dreaded draughts. Given that it blows a cold draught, AirCon isn't very popular in Germany, despite Germany having fairly warm summers. Most people just tilt the window in slightly (known as Fenster auf Kipp). Leaving the window open like this has led to a new phenomenon: Kippfenster-syndrome . This describes anything, usually cats although it could apply to burglars as well, that try to sneak in through the tilted window and end up getting stuck.

Between all the different ailments that you can succumb to and the confusing relationship with the air, It's fair to say that Germans can be fanatical about their health. It's one of the reasons bio food is so popular in Germany, considerably more popular than most other European countries. The demand is so high that even the discount supermarkets have started lines to cater for the demand, stocking organic fruit and vegetables, along with some very German-sounding health juices like beetroot and sauerkraut juice.

Given the stereotype that Germans are logical and practical, it's hard for foreigners to get their heads around German hypochondria. It's even more baffling when Germans explain the benefits of bio food or the reasons that you should close the window, all the while puffing on a cigarette.

The answer to why Germans are always monitoring their health and immediately coming down with illnesses might be the doctor's waiting room. In waiting rooms in the rest of the world, people tend to keep to themselves and either play on their phones or read one of the many out-of-date magazines on the table. It's rare to pay much attention to someone else in the waiting room, let alone speak to them.

In Germany, things are surprisingly friendlier. Enter the waiting room and all the other patients will greet you with a friendly "Guten Tag" or "Hallo." Then, when you leave everyone will say "Auf Wiedersehen" to you as well.

There are very few parts of German society that are this friendly, and so it's little wonder that everyone's constantly coming down with something and rushing off to see the doctor.

Travel

32
GO TO MALLE EVERY SUMMER

Every year millions of Germans pack their bags and head off to Mallorca to enjoy the holiday that they booked the year before. It doesn't matter whether you're the kind of German who likes to drink Sangria from a bucket or the kind who likes to stay in five-star hotels. Mallorca is just where you'll go. For whatever reason, Germans feel this incredible connection with the island and come back to it year after year.

Mallorca (often referred to as Malle in Germany) is so popular with the Germans that it's often referred to as the 17th federal state of Germany. It's a place where there are beautiful (and free) beaches, palm trees, and where the sun always shines. Of course, there are plenty of places like this around both Spain and the rest of the world, but what makes Malle so special is that while having all of these things, it's still fairly German as well.

The staff in the hotels and resorts all speak German, play German music, and some even serve German food. It's also a part of Spain where it's relatively easy to get hold of German essentials like brown bread, or have your beer served in a German Stein glass.

For Germans, Malle is a time for hedonism, whether that means partying and hangovers or just eating good food, relaxing in the sun, and taking afternoon naps. All of this is a one-off, something that can only happen in Malle. There's even a famous German song about it: "Malle ist nur einmal im Jahr... " (Malle is just once a year.)

33
IDOLISE SCANDINAVIA

Bullerbü-Syndrom is the notion that Scandinavia is utopia and it's a popular way of thinking in Germany. Scandinavia - Sweden, in particular - is a lot like Germany but better. In Sweden the people are blonder, richer, friendlier, better educated, and everything runs more efficiently. Sweden is essentially a German's wet dream.

Very few people have written about Bullerbü-Syndrom, but considering most German children grow up reading the stories of Swedish author Astrid Lindgren, it's probably something Germans develop at an early age.

Of course, whether or not Sweden is actually paradise is up for debate, but Sweden isn't going to argue, particularly because Bullerbü-Syndrom is responsible for so much of their tourism. Every summer, Swedish roads are packed with German cars as they head north in search of a little slice of Scandi utopia.

This tourism doesn't come for free. When the Germans appear, moose road signs disappear. Every summer, hundreds of these signposts go missing. To Germans, these signposts are more Swedish than anything you will find in a souvenir shop and even though stealing one means breaking a big rule, this is one they're willing to break if it means their homes can have a small reminder of the utopia that is Sweden.

34
GET NAKED WHEN IT GETS WARM

Nudism is a part of Germany's *Freikörperkultur* (free body culture), a movement that dates back as far as the 19th century. Unlike America and Britain, where nudism is generally considered a taboo, in Germany it's just a part of life. Go to a park or beach during the summer time, flick on your television in the evening, or walk into your local sauna, and you're bound to see a few naked Germans.

Although Freikörperkultur (or FKK) was initially popular for its health benefits, over the course of the 20th-century nudism gained a political motive as well, making it even more popular. The Nazis tried to ban it in the 1930s, and even succeeded for a couple of months, but even the Third Reich wasn't strong enough to stop Germans from whipping their bits out in public. They finally reached a compromise, only banning communists and homosexuals from joining in. This factoid is best not mentioned in German company, however: see the chapter 'Don't Make Nazi Jokes'.

When the wall went up, and East and West Germany were divided, nudism became even more popular in the communist east. Getting naked gave people a sense of liberty in what was otherwise an oppressive society. Since the fall of the Berlin Wall, FKK has decreased in popularity; at least in terms of membership to nudist clubs.

Today, German nudists are split into two groups. Firstly, there are the ones who just like to take their clothes off when it gets warm so that they don't end up with tan lines. Then there are the committed nudists, who are usually older and part of a nudist organisation. Most nudist organisations just hang about naked at their beach and lake clubs, but for the more adventurous, there are nudist hiking and even Frisbee groups.

Nudism may be on the decline, but it's not disappeared yet. Go to a German beach, lake, the Tiergarten in the centre of Berlin or the Englischer Garten in the centre of Munich, and you'll see plenty of evidence that it's still very much a popular German pastime.

35
PAY TO GO ON THE BEACH

Beaches aren't something that you would normally associate with Germany, but Northern Germany is famous for its beautiful coastline, in Germany at least. Every year millions of Germans take their Audis and BMWs and race north along the autobahns for a little bit of sun, sea, and sand.

That Germans love the beach is a well-known fact. They're a frequent sight on beaches all over Europe, often identifiable by the sock and sandals combo. They're also the most likely ones to be walking around in the nude. Germans love the beach so much that they build artificial beaches wherever possible. By the lake or on the roof of multi-storey car parks are two of the most popular locations.

But even though Germans love all beaches, they have a particular affinity for their own. They love their beaches so much that they've even written pop songs about them. In 1985, pop duo Klaus und Klaus took the Irish drinking song The Wild Rover and re-wrote it so it had absolutely nothing to do with drunken debauchery and instead focused on just how wonderful the NordseeKüste (North Sea coast) is. The song, An der Nordseeküste, is an ode to the tides, fish, and dykes that make the North Sea coast so special. It was a big hit in Germany, selling close to a million copies.

German beaches may be beautiful, and let's not forget that the entire coastline has a theme song, but what makes these beaches undeniably German is the little bit of bureaucracy that you have to go through to go to the beach. Try to get onto the beach in Germany and you'll be asked to pay a Kurtaxe: an entry fee that's somewhere in the region of 5-15 Euro. This fee goes towards the upkeep of the beach and is just one of the many small taxes that Germans have to pay.

Unfortunately, getting onto the beach doesn't mean the end of bureaucracy. Depending on which beach you go to, there are many rules and regulations to be aware of. On the island of Sylt, in the North Sea, sandcastles are completely banned, while in Neustadt and Sierksdorf they are only allowed so long as they don't have a diameter greater than four metres. In Kellenhusen and Großenbrode, no sandcastle may be greater than fifty centimetres in height.

Considering all of these rules, it's no surprise that millions of Germans jet off to more laid-back beaches in places like Mallorca every single year.

36
DIG A HOLE WHEN YOU GO ON THE BEACH

As we've already mentioned, Germans can be spotted on beaches throughout Europe. As a result, every European country has its own opinion about what the Germans get up to on holiday.

Ask an English holidaymaker and he'll wax lyrical about sun loungers and how he can never get one because the Germans get up first thing in the morning to reserve the best ones with their beach towels. The fashion-conscious Italians will mention the socks and sandals combo Germans are so famous for wearing. Ask the Dutch, however, and they'll tell you that when the Germans go to the beach they like to dig holes.

Nobody quite knows how this particular stereotype came to be, but the Dutch are adamant it's true. They're quite possibly correct as well. In 2010, a German tourist staying in Tenerife had to be rescued by firefighters after the tunnel system he'd built to connect two three-metre deep holes collapsed around him, trapping him up to his neck in sand.

If the Dutch jokes that followed are anything to go by, this unusual obsession is because Germans can't switch off on holidays; especially when there's a little engineering work to be done.

Whatever the reason, this news story isn't the only evidence to suggest it's true. At the German seaside resort of St. Peter-Ording in Schleswig-Holstein, digger trucks can be seen early every morning – even earlier than the sun lounger snatchers – filling in the holes that have been dug on the beach the day before.

Sex & Romance

"Mrs Robinson, You're trying to seduce me. Aren't you?"

"I think we're at the stage where you can use the 'du' form, don't you?"

37
FLIRT AS INCONSPICUOUSLY AS YOU CAN

Flirting with Germans can be frustrating for foreigners, regardless of whether you're a man or a woman. Most Germans are fairly reserved when it comes to flirting. Eye contact is seen as a big deal, and even then it's not always accompanied with a smile.

Tips for Men
German women aren't used to a forward approach as German men tend to be shy and aren't good at initiating contact unless they're drunk.

If you're confident in your flirting abilities you may think that this is a good opportunity for you to jump in, but be careful: being too forward can backfire. Act too friendly and use obvious chat-up lines and that lovely Fräulein will put up a wall. Less is more here.

Tips for Women
Compared to British and American men, German men are shy. They'll make eye contact and maybe even smile if you're lucky. If you expect them to be braver than that by, say, coming over and talking to you, you might end up disappointed. Give them a little hand. Don't be afraid to wander over and break the ice: just don't be too full-on or you might scare him off.

38
CHOOSE A GOOD NIGHT'S SLEEP OVER ROMANCE

Germans have a reputation for being the least romantic nation, and the most practical. There's no greater example of this than the double bed you'll find in most hotels, apartment rentals, and homes in Germany.

Instead of a double mattress with a double duvet, German beds are made up of two single mattresses with separate duvets. Snuggling up under the covers isn't easy, and this system leaves a gap between the beds. On the plus side, however, if one of you moves around in their sleep or is a duvet hog, the other person won't be disturbed. You also get to choose different mattresses, so one person can have a hard mattress and the other a soft, depending on each person's preference. It's not the most romantic way to share a bed but in terms of quality of sleep it's certainly the most efficient.

While many non-Germans quickly convert to the German double bed, few ever adjust to the pillows. German pillows are big and square as opposed to the rectangular shape that most of us are used to. They're also fairly flimsy and in order to give your head the same level of support that a standard rectangular pillow would, most people have to fold them over.

What's funny is that despite German pillows being more like a paper napkin than a pillow, in Germany a pillow is classified as a "passive weapon". Hitting someone over the head with one can lead to being charged with assault.

39
WATCH GERMAN PORN

Along with cars and bread, Germany has built an international reputation for its porn. So famous that it's become a bit of a running joke within Hollywood. Porn scenes in comedy movies are chock full of actors attempting German accents for a laugh, for example the infamous scene with Cartman's Mom in the South Park Movie. But ask most Germans about their country's porn industry and you will get quite a few blank stares.

Germany has been successfully producing porn since the late 1960s and remains a major producer today. With its lax laws for porn production, this has attracted both big producers and also small businesses and startups as well. Many of these companies have tried to corner a niche market such as gangbangs, or urine and faecal porn. They've evidently been quite successful as the latter is now commonly referred to as Scheisse Porn.

Do those blank stares mean that Germans are genuinely unaware? It's hard to say. According to research by Pornhub, one of the world's largest porn websites, 50% of searches originating in Germany contain the word "Deutsch" or "German". Of those that do visit sites like Pornhub there's definitely a trend towards German-made porn, but it's possible that a good proportion of the population is also unaware.

It's probably not worth educating them either. Although

Germans are typically very proud of German-made products and successful small German businesses, complimenting them on their porn industry probably isn't the best conversation starter. A much better idea would be to compliment them on cuckoo clocks instead.

40
TREAT PROSTITUTION LIKE ANY OTHER JOB

Think of prostitutes and Amsterdam will probably spring to mind. But although the capital of Holland is famous for being Europe's capital of debauchery, few people know that prostitution is also legal in Germany.

Like all industries in Germany, brothels are regulated. For starters, prostitutes pay income tax and charge VAT for their services. Paying into the system means they're eligible for health care as well. They can even earn diplomas thanks to a new scheme aimed at training sex workers on the best way to serve disabled clients. And to help curb trafficking, women from outside the EU need to obtain a working visa if they want to have sex in exchange for money.

In Bonn, the capital of former West Germany, street-walkers purchase tickets in the same way as you would a parking ticket. This allows them to 'park' themselves and do business. Several cities, including Bonn, have also introduced drive-thru areas, essentially garages where Johns can take their hookers to do the deed.

Germany's attitude is surely it's better to legalise and regulate it? Not only can you collect taxes, but the government can look after the well-being of the sex workers as well.

41
SHOW UP ON TIME FOR YOUR WEDDING

Despite the nudism, pornography, and legal prostitution in Germany, and despite the challenges that go with flirting, Cupid does manage to hit a few Germans with his arrows every year. If he does, and it all works out, a good proportion of Germans decide to get married.

Given that Germans aren't known for being particularly romantic, and legal assistance insurance (Rechtschutz-versicherung) doesn't cover divorce, those superstitious Germans have come up with some traditions to ensure the bride and groom live happily ever after.

Before the ceremony

The bride's shoes
Traditionally at least, German women look forward to their wedding day their entire lives. This gives them plenty of time to put aside some money for the big day, which they start doing as little girls. This money goes towards covering the cost of the shoes they'll wear on the wedding day.

When the day comes to buy the shoes, the bride will pay for them with all of the change that she's saved up over the years. This is supposed to indicate that she's frugal and a good saver. After all, isn't that what every man looks for in a woman?

These days most women don't start saving when they're children, or if they do, they don't keep saving throughout their lives. It's still traditional to pay for the shoes with coins, but these tend to come from family and friends and not from the bride's life savings.

The night before
The Polterabend, or the night before the wedding, is traditionally spent smashing porcelain in an attempt to make enough noise to scare off any evil spirits that might harm the marriage. Don't make the mistake of breaking glass as this is considered bad luck (the breaking of the glass that is, not the fact that you're destroying someone's kitchen).

After all of the family, friends and wedding guests have worked their way through the couple's fine china, the couple is then left to clean it up together. This symbolises their ability to work together, which is the key to a happy marriage.

The morning of the wedding
After cleaning up the remnants of what were her favourite plates, the bride heads off to spend the night at her parent's home. Traditionally, this is the last night she would spend there.

In the morning, it's customary for her friends to run into her bedroom shouting, screaming, and letting off firecrackers to wake her up. Some people even take it to entire new extremes and bring in marching bands or gun clubs to help heighten the noise.

During the ceremony

Walking down the aisle
Traditionally the bride and groom walk down the aisle together. This way the bride can't leave her future husband sweating it out at the altar wondering if she's going to turn up

or not. Sadly for German grooms, modern German weddings have been influenced by American films. It's controversial, but it's becoming more and more common for the bride to walk down the aisle with her father and to be a few minutes late.

Coin in the bride's shoe
Traditionally, the bride keeps a coin in her shoe during the ceremony. This superstition is meant to keep the marriage free from financial trouble. In practice, it tends to result in blisters, and so nowadays most brides find ways of attaching the coin to the outside of the shoe rather than putting it inside.

The shoe often makes another appearance later on in the wedding where it's auctioned off. All of the guests bid on it; although it's always the groom who should offer the highest bid. He'll then give his wife back her shoe but collect all of the other bids, which the lucky couple get to keep.

After the Ceremony
The motorcade
After the ceremony, the bride and groom are driven about town in an expensive car while the rest of the party drives behind honking their horns.

Veil dance
If you want to dance with the bride or groom at their wedding, you will have to pay for it. It may seem cunningly enterprising of the couple, but as you'll see in the next tradition, this money often finds its way back to the guests at the party, and it's more likely just a way for the couple to break even.

Kidnapping of the bride
A historic German tradition involves the groom kidnapping the bride on the night of their wedding so that they can spend the night together. These days the tradition has changed. Now the friends of the bride kidnap her instead. The groom has to run around town, hunting in all of the local pubs until he finds

her.

The couple has the rest of their lives to spend together, so it often surprises outsiders when they see a groom hunting so intensely. This has nothing to do with romance. The groom needs to find her quickly as he's responsible for paying the bar tab for the bride and her kidnappers. Considering how much Germans love beer, the bill can add up quickly!

First night
The groom's troubles aren't quite over yet. Traditionally, friends of the couple like to play one last prank by messing up the couple's apartment. It's common for the bride and groom to come home to find the bed taken apart and important items such as toothbrushes and condoms hidden. It's also common to set and hide as many alarm clocks as possible. This ensures that what should already have been a pretty memorable night definitely is.

The morning after

The next morning it is customary for the groom to present the bride with a small gift. Traditionally it's jewellery or money, but these days it's usually something smaller and simpler. Probably because he's had to spend all of his money replacing their fine china and paying for her friends' bar tab. Although it's not traditional, the bride often has something for the groom as well.

Plant a tree
Finally, if you want to ensure that your marriage is a healthy one, plant a tree. Germans believe this brings good luck to the marriage. Apple trees represent fertility, which is quite ominous if your friends hid your condoms the night before while oak trees represent a steady marriage.

Food & Drink

42
KNOW YOUR SAUSAGES

Despite global health concerns over processed meat, Germans still love a good sausage. It's probably the most German food you can eat if they leave any for you that is. Yes, Germans love their 1,200 different varieties of sausage so much that they each consume an average of 30kg of sausage a year. That's around 2.5 million tons in total, roughly half the annual amount of meat consumed in Germany.

Although the Germans have more types of sausage than Eskimos have words for snow, you probably will struggle to try all 1,200 of them. Not just because it would take you a seriously long time to do so, or that you might have a heart attack in the process, but because some sausages are quite hard to find.

Some are regional while others only tend to make an appearance at certain times of the year. Bremen's Pinkel sausage, for example, is normally eaten with Grünkohl or Braunkohl (both types of kale) during the winter months when kale comes into season.

But of all the 1,200 different German sausages, the most famous has to be the Currywurst. A Currywurst is a sliced Bratwurst seasoned with Currywurst sauce and served with bread or French fries. It can be ordered with skin (Currywurst mit Darm) or without (Darmlos). East Berliners tend to eat it without the skin, whereas West Berliners prefer the skin. There aren't any hard and fast rules; it's more a matter of personal preference.

The story behind the invention of the Currywurst goes something like this. In 1949, Herta Heuwer, a German living in Berlin, borrowed ketchup and curry powder from some British soldiers. She mixed the two together and voilà, German gastronomy has never been the same again.

Heuwer started selling the sausages from a small snack stand in the Charlottenburg district, and they quickly became a huge hit with the construction workers who were rebuilding the ruined city. At the height of its popularity, the stand was selling around ten thousand portions of Currywurst a week.

It isn't just construction workers that like Currywurst either. Former German Chancellor Gerhard Schröder is a fan, although his former and vegetarian wife Hillu, was not. Luckily for Schröder there was a Currywurst stand on his way to work, safely out of view of his house. Including Schröder's daily consumption, the Deutsches Currywurst Museum estimates that around 800 million Currywurst are eaten every year in Germany, with over 70 million eaten in Berlin alone. There is even (and nobody is quite sure why) a currywurst-flavoured energy drink.

Along with the Currywurst, there are many other sausages worth trying. These are all available throughout the year and the whole of the country as well.

Bockwurst - Traditionally eaten alongside a Bock beer during the springtime, Bockwurst is a parsley-flavoured sausage that's usually served with mustard.
Blutwurst - Made from congealed blood and mixed with oatmeal and spices, Blutwurst is similar to the black pudding found in the UK and Ireland.
Weisswurst - Boiled Bavarian veal and pork sausages, these are

often eaten during Oktoberfest. Along with Weissbier, pretzels, and sweet mustard they're an important part of the Bavarian breakfast. There's a saying that weisswurst should never hear the noon bells toll, as in times gone by the fresh sausages would be at their best before midday.

43
EAT A BIG GERMAN BREAKFAST

Germans like to go all out when it comes to breakfast, although these days this is mainly just on the weekend. Smaller breakfasts are commonplace on weekdays. A traditional German breakfast is made up of jams and honey, Frischkäse (cream cheese), eggs, cheeses, fruit and vegetables, smoked fish, meats and sausages. There aren't any hard and fast rules as to what your German breakfast should contain, except that it should be plentiful, filling, and contain lots and lots of bread.

Germans are very proud of their breads of which there are over 1,300 different types. German bread is typically dark and malty, packed with seeds and grains, and useful if you ever need to remove one of your teeth. While white bread does exist in Germany, it is often looked down upon as being soft, tender, and very unhealthy in comparison to the far superior brown bread.

Bread is a big part of a German breakfast, and it usually makes an appearance at just about every other meal as well. At school, German children have another meal to keep them going in between breakfast and lunch: the Pausenbrot (bread break) or Zweites Frühstück (second breakfast). Adults also often take a break for a Zwischenmahlzeit (in between meal time) or Brotzeit (bread time).

Then there's lunch, the main meal of the day, which is usually hot and doesn't necessarily include bread, although plenty of people have some on the side.

Once they get home from work and school, Germans have their evening meal, Abendbrot (evening bread), which is exactly that: an evening meal consisting of bread, cheeses and hams.

When in Germany, be sure to order "real" German bread and none of that soft, fluffy, and unhealthy white stuff.

44
EAT DÖNER KEBABS (EVEN SOBER)

If you've ever visited Berlin, you'll understand the city's obsession with kebabs. It's not surprising when you understand that Berlin invented the Döner Kebab, or at least it's the city that's given credit for its invention. In particular, credit goes to Kadir Nurman, a Turkish immigrant who moved to Berlin and set up a stall in the 1970s.

Nurman wasn't the first person to think of grilling meat, or even grilling meat on a pole, but he claims he was the first person to think of shaving chunks of it off and stuffing it in a sandwich. Although many other people have made the same claim, in 2011 Nurman's contribution was finally recognised by the Association of Turkish Döner Manufacturers (basically the Oscars for grilled meat sellers).

Today the Döner is one of Germany's most popular fast foods and, along with Currywurst and Apfelschorle; it's one of those quintessential foods that you should try when in Germany. High competition between Döner stands means the quality in Germany is considerably higher than in other countries, or in more practical terms: they're not just for soaking up alcohol, you can eat them sober. Kebabs are enjoyed by just about everyone in Germany, right up the social ladder to the elite. There's even a kebab shop near the Federal Ministry of Finance in Berlin that claims to be a favourite lunch spot of Angela Merkel. Venture further south in the city, to the district of Kreuzberg, and you'll find Kottiwood, a kebab shop John F.

Kennedy visited while in the city to deliver his "Ich bin ein Berliner" speech.

There are also some interesting variations on the classic kebab to try. One of the best is the Döner Gemüse Kebab, a kebab topped with roasted vegetables (usually carrot, potato, peppers, aubergine, and courgette). Mustafa's Gemüse Kebab on the capital's Mehringdamm is one of the most popular places to try this, but be prepared to queue for up to an hour.

45
BRING KARTOFFELSALAT TO ANY EVENT

Just about every meal in Germany comes with potatoes, for example Currywurst comes with French fries while Schnitzel is usually served with pan-fried potatoes (Bratkartoffeln). Potatoes also come mashed (Kartoffelbrei), baked (Ofenkartoffel), boiled and salted (Salzkartoffeln), and as pancakes (Kartoffelpuffer). It's funny to think then that, according to legend at least, the potato had a hard time finding acceptance in Germany.

According to the story, when explorers brought the potato back to Europe, King Frederick II of Prussia tried to encourage peasants to plant it. The potato, he believed, could be a cheap source of nutrition and could help lower the price of other essentials like bread.

In 1774 during a famine, Frederick even offered free potatoes to the peasants, but they turned him down saying: "The things have neither smell nor taste, not even the dogs will eat them, so what use are they to us?" Angry, initially Frederick's response was to threaten to cut the nose and ears off any peasant that refused to eat potatoes, but after cooling down he decided to use a little reverse psychology instead. He planted a field of potatoes, told the peasants that they couldn't have them anymore, and put guards around it, quietly telling them not to guard it at all.

Seeing the guards around the potato field made the peasants want the potatoes, and they began breaking into the field and stealing them. It wasn't long before they began replanting them and Frederick got what he wanted.

These days just about every German dish is served with potatoes, and the nation's favourite dish, or at least one that's definitely in the running for the title, Kartoffelsalat, is made almost entirely of potatoes.

Traditionally, a German Kartoffelsalat includes bacon, red onion, vinegar, and herbs, although there are several takes on the traditional recipe. Unlike American potato salad, the German version doesn't traditionally use mayonnaise.

Go to any potluck or picnic in Germany, and pretty much everyone invited will have brought potato salad. In fact, potato salad will make an appearance at just about every event you attend in Germany. Although this does mean you'll very quickly start to grow tired of it, it's worth realising that Kartoffelsalat is considerably better than the other German take on the salad: Wurstsalat (sausage salad).

46
GET EXCITED ABOUT ASPARAGUS SEASON

Germans look forward to the start of Spargelzeit (asparagus season) with the same excitement that the residents of Punxsutawney, Pennsylvania look forward to Groundhog Day. Spargel is the first fresh vegetable of spring, and like the Groundhog making an appearance, it's a sign that winter is finally over.

Spargel is an unusual German obsession, one that can take many years of living in Germany to understand. Even then you'll wonder if you're genuinely as excited as everyone else.

During Spargel season (April-July) just about every menu in Germany will feature at least one asparagus-based dish on it. Many traditional German restaurants will have an entire menu dedicated to asparagus dishes. White asparagus is most common, as Germans see it as superior to green asparagus.

This obsession is so great that, as well as having entire menus dedicated to it, there are also Spargel festivals, Spargel peeling contests, and in Beelitz there's an annual beauty pageant to see who will win the crown and become the asparagus queen. Once asparagus season is over, there's the mushroom and strawberry season to look forward to as well.

47
HAVE A HOT LUNCH & A COLD DINNER

Germans traditionally eat their main, hot meal at lunchtime and have a cold meal (Abendbrot) in the evening. Abendbrot means 'evening bread' and usually consists of bread with ham, cheese, dips, and some veggies. As with all mealtimes in Germany, this is normally eaten at the table rather than in front of the TV.

The practice of eating a hot lunch and a cold dinner most likely comes from the days when the majority of people worked in agricultural or manual jobs. They needed a high number of calories to work in the afternoon, having already burnt off the calories of the large German breakfast that they'd eaten earlier that morning.

Although times have changed considerably, having a hot lunch and a cold dinner is still common in Germany. Almost every workplace, regardless of whether it's a big or a small company, will have a canteen to provide German workers with their daily hot lunch.

Lunchtime, particularly in offices, tends to be on the dot at twelve and usually there will be a stampede to the canteen at this point. If you meet anyone coming the other way, it's custom to say "Mahlzeit" (meal time or 'time to eat') as opposed to "Hallo" or "Guten Tag." This is presumably just in case anyone thinks it would be a good opportunity to experiment with the ins and outs of chit-chat.

In smaller towns, you'll find most places shut while people go home or to the canteen for their hot lunch. And regardless of where you are, all the government offices will probably be closed for lunch as well.

48
SHARE A BAG OF DOUGHNUTS WITH FRIENDS

A Berliner is a traditional German doughnut that's filled with jam or marmalade and dusted with powdered sugar. Unlike American doughnuts, there is no hole in the middle of a Berliner.

Although Berliners are available every day of the year, it's traditional to eat them on Silvester (New Year's Eve) as well as on the Carnival holidays Rosenmontag (Shrove Monday) and Fastnachtsdienstag (Shrove Tuesday). A popular prank is to fill one Berliner with mustard, hand out the doughnuts to your friends, and see who starts crying first. And they say Germans don't have a sense of humour!

According to popular legend, when John F. Kennedy uttered the famous words "Ich bin ein Berliner" he called himself a jelly doughnut. As funny as that would have been, this is nothing but an urban legend. If JFK had said "Ich bin Berliner" ("I am a citizen of Berlin") people would have laughed at him. With that American accent, who is going to believe that he's a Berlin native? Although "Ich bin ein Berliner" could be translated as I am a jelly doughnut in other parts of Germany, the translation doesn't apply when speaking to a group of people from Berlin. While jelly doughnuts are called Berliners in the rest of Germany, in Berlin they're called Pfannkuchen (pancakes). It's not surprising that his German was correct. As president of the USA, it's more than likely that

a native German speaker helped him with his speech
beforehand.

49
DON'T EXPECT YOUR WATER TO BE ANYTHING BUT SPARKLING

Ask for water in a restaurant in Germany and the waiter will bring you a bottle of sparkling water. It isn't that the waiter is trying to sell you a more expensive bottle, or that German tap water isn't drinkable. You can order tap water (Leitungswasser), but in Germany people tend to like a bit of fizz in anything they drink, whether it's apple juice or water.

Sparkling water even has different levels of carbonation: Klassisch is heavily carbonated, Medium is slightly carbonated while still is either non-carbonated or very slightly sparkling. The Germans enjoy carbonated water so much that still water is anything below 5.5g of carbon dioxide per litre. The only way you're guaranteed will be completely still is if you drink it from the tap.

One of the easiest faux pas you can make in Germany is offering someone a glass of still water. Many German households have home carbonators (such as a SodaStream) so that they never find themselves in the awkward social situation of only having still water to offer guests.

50
EXPERIMENT WITH NEW DRINK MIXES

Germans are rarely content to settle on drinking a simple coke or lemonade. Not when there are new, undiscovered flavours out there. These days someone has tried almost every combination and so some of the newer combinations are experimental to say the least.

The following are some of Germany's favourite drink mixes and are widely considered to be a success. Whether you agree is another story, but it's worth trying a few to see what this particular obsession is all about.

Spezi - Fanta mixed with cola.
Radler – Beer and lemonade (shandy).
Maracujaschorle - Passion fruit and sparkling water.
Johannisbeerschorle - Blackcurrant and sparkling water.
Diesel - Beer and Cola.
Kiba - Cherry juice and banana juice.
Schorle - Fruit juice mixed with sparkling water. There are countless variations of this. Apfelschorle (apple) and Rhabarberschorle (rhubarb) are two of the most popular flavours.
Weinschorle - White wine and sparkling water or lemonade.
Cola-Weizen - Cola and wheat beer.
Kalte Muschi - Red wine and coke.

These days just about every combination has been through the testing process. Apfelschorle is generally the most popular while Orangenschorle is the least. Most of these flavours are available already made up at convenience stores, cafés, and restaurants. If you can't find the flavour you're looking for, it's pretty simple to make them up at home.

If you aren't ready to become a Schorle mixologist, Germany has a few native soft drinks that are worth trying. In particular, Club Mate, which is Germany's answer to energy drinks like Red Bull and Monster. As expected from a modern German product, it's far more health conscious. It's high in caffeine but doesn't have the insanely high sugar levels associated with energy drinks.

For whatever reason, the producers of Club Mate never did any advertising, and it never gained the same popularity that Fanta did. It wasn't until the 2000s when Berlin's tech scene began to boom that Germany discovered its native, low-calorie, high caffeine drink. It's the perfect fuel for late-night hackathons, and it's also a popular tipple in all-night techno clubs like Berghain.

Walk around Germany in the summer and you'll see plenty of people with either a bottle of Club Mate or some variation of Schorle in their hands. Both are worth trying, either pure or as part of an alcoholic cocktail.

Of course, Club Mate isn't Germany's most successful homegrown drink. That title goes to Fanta. Invented in Nazi Germany, Fanta came about when a US trade embargo made it difficult for Germany to import Coca-Cola syrup. The German head of Coca-Cola decided to create his own product, Fanta, with ingredients that were only available in Germany at that time. Since then Fanta has become one of the best-selling soft drinks worldwide and a major alternative to Coca-Cola.

51
DRINK BIER, AND LOTS OF IT

Germany tops the tables for many things – football, recycling, productivity, you name it – and they manage to do it all while remaining one of the top beer-consuming nations in the world. Germans love beer, and they love to drink an awful lot of it as well, particularly during Oktoberfest where it's drunk a litre at a time.

While wine is also popular, and alcopops and other international drinks have found a market in Germany, beer is still by far the favourite alcoholic drink. It's sometimes cheaper than water and almost always cheaper than wine, especially in restaurants. You'll find beer everywhere: at McDonalds, in movie theatres, and even the fridge in motorway service stations. In Bavaria, they drink Hefeweizen beer at breakfast time, although these days it's usually just for brunch at the weekend (Frühschoppen). The German language really does have a word for everything, even getting together with friends and drinking before midday.

Despite the low-cost, if it's German you can bet it's good quality. Like everything else in Germany, the beer industry is heavily regulated. In fact, the German government have regulated beer production for centuries. In 1516, Bavaria (and later the rest of Germany) passed the Reinheitsgebot law. It states that only barley, hops, and water can be used to make beer, although it was later updated to include yeast as well. The law was designed to hold the beer industry to high standards and was one of Germany's first attempts at regulating the food and drink industry. Since then, Germans have enjoyed high-quality beer as well as regulating just about every other area of life as well. Although Germany updated the Reinheitsgebot to be less stringent in 1993, most German brewers continue to follow the original, stricter law voluntarily.

When it comes time to order a beer in Germany, you'll find there are a lot of different options. There are more than five thousand types of beer in Germany, but these are some of the most popular:

Pils - A pale lager from Czech Bohemia and the most common type of beer in Germany.
Altbier - A popular top-fermented beer from Düsseldorf. Only ten breweries currently produce it.
Kölsch - A straw-yellow hue, similar to pale lager but fruitier, from Cologne.
Helles Lager - A pale lager from Bavaria, similar to Pils.
Lager Dunkel, Dunkles - Malty, dark beers.
Bockbier, Starkbier - Lager with a higher alcohol content.
Berliner Weisse - A white beer with a low alcohol content that's popular in Berlin. It's often mixed with woodruff (Waldmeister) or raspberry syrup for a summer drink.
Weizenbier/Weissbier - A top-fermented wheat beer that's particularly popular in Bavaria.

Tip I: Ordering beer
When ordering a beer, use your thumb as opposed to your index finger to show that you want one beer. In Germany, the index finger is your second finger and holding this finger up will probably result in you getting two beers. Of course this isn't necessarily a bad thing, especially if it is breakfast time in Bavaria. Prost!

Tip II: Say prost!
While we're on the subject of Prost (cheers), it's important that

you cheer correctly. What's important here isn't so much that you remember to say it in German. Most Germans will forgive you for saying cheers instead of Prost. They won't forgive you for not looking deep into their eyes when you say it, however.

Germans, as we've mentioned before, are superstitious. Not looking into the other person's eyes when saying Prost will apparently bring seven years of bad sex. As Germany rarely tops the table for the most romantic nation in the world, they're very keen to avoid that!

German Calendar

52
RIOT ON THE 1ST OF MAY

Since 1987, it's been traditional to have a good old-fashioned riot on International Worker's Day. The most famous riots take place in Berlin's Kreuzberg district and feature some store plundering, the odd brick thrown here and there (normally in the direction of the police), and the occasional burnt offering of someone's car.

The police like to get involved as well, just like the good old days when hippy-bashings were much more frequent. May 1st is a good opportunity to don their riot gear and test out the new water cannons and pepper sprays. You can often see groups of police officers stationed on side streets, lazily flipping through paperbacks just waiting for the command to get down to business.

The first May Day riot in Kreuzberg took place in 1987 when civilian unrest drove the police out of the SO36 postcode for several hours. Protesters used cars to create flaming barricades on Oranienstrasse, looted over 30 shops, and set the Gorlitzer Bahnhof train station on fire. The next day the protesters slept off their hangovers in jail while everyone else tidied up their mess.

Germans love a tradition, and every year since then Berlin's far left, socialist, and anti-fascist groups have tried to recreate the drama of the first Kreuzberg riot. Sadly, like most things in Berlin, even the riots haven't been able to avoid gentrification.

These days more people take to the streets for the street parties rather than to lob bricks at the police. That said, the banks and shops in Kreuzberg still board up their windows on 30th April, just in case.

Jealous that Berlin was having all the fun, Hamburg started its own annual riot in the Schanzenviertel neighbourhood. For those who think the 1st of May riots in Berlin are "so over", Hamburg promises those classic police and protester battles like Berlin used to have.

The 2nd of May is usually a quiet day. There are hangovers and black eyes to nurse before both sides take turns at pointing the finger and arguing over who started it. Secretly though, everybody is counting down the days to next year so they can do the whole thing all over again.

53
LIGHT A FIRE FOR OSTERN (EASTER)

Easter in Germany is a chocolate-filled celebration. Everyone gets their dose of Milka and Lindt in the form of Easter eggs, bunnies, and other chocolate goodies. For parents, it's a chance to get a few hours of peace and quiet: most hide the eggs and send the children outside to go looking for them. Then there are the Osterfeuer (Easter Fires).

Osterfeuer are big open fires. These range from small fires in people's gardens to big community organised bonfires accompanied by drinks, music, and food.

Like many European celebrations, Osterfeuer are pagan in origin. The Christians adopted them sometime around 1500 AD, declaring them to no longer be pagan but a symbol of God's light in the world. Osterfeuer are also popular in Scandinavia, the Netherlands, Austria and Switzerland. In some parts of Germany it's common to burn Judas puppets.

If you're in Germany during Easter, don't miss out on the chance to celebrate with a bottle of schnapps while dancing around a big open fire. Like all German events where there's alcohol, it's a good opportunity to make friends and get to know people. Or, if you've overindulged during Easter, it's a chance to burn off some of that chocolate.

54
GET DRUNK ON FATHER'S DAY

In most countries, Father's Day is a day when dad gets to put his feet up and enjoy breakfast in bed while the children mow the lawn, take out the rubbish, and do all the other chores that dad normally has to do.

In Germany, it's a little bit different. Although Vatertag started off in the same vein as Father's Day in other countries, sometime around the end of the 19th century some German dads decided that breakfast in bed wasn't really for them. Instead, what they wanted to do is walk around town pulling a big cart (Bollerwagen) filled with bottles of beer. As the day goes on, the carts get a little lighter, and the dads considerably more intoxicated. This leads to singing and dancing as well as challenges that revolve around who can finish their beer the fastest.

These days some dads have opted for the lower-key, more sober version of Father's Day. Their places were quickly filled by men without children, which is why some people refer to the event as Herrentag (Men's Day) instead. Even women have started to get involved, and we can't blame them either. The female equivalent, Muttertag, is more about flowers and chocolate and is much too tame for some German women.

55
GET REALLY DRUNK ON OKTOBERFEST

Of all the German festivals, Oktoberfest is by far the most well-known and the most important, from an international perspective at least. You've probably already heard of it, or been to some kind of Oktoberfest celebration.

Oktoberfest is a 16-day event that dates back to 1810 when Prince Ludwig married Princess Therese. Feeling generous, the Prince and Princess invited Munich's citizens to join in the celebrations, held in a field just outside the city gates. The meadow, Theresienwiese, is where Munich celebrates Oktoberfest to this day. While you'll find small Oktoberfest celebrations in cities like Berlin, Hamburg and Frankfurt, and even the very large Volksfest in Stuttgart, Munich is still home to the biggest and most popular festival in the country.

Although Oktoberfest is an October festival, in true German fashion it actually starts at the end of September. This gives attendees a better chance of good weather and slightly longer evenings, as the German weather goes from bad to worse.

At Oktoberfest, you'll have a chance to drink Bavaria's finest produce one litre at a time, often while standing on the top of a table and singing along to German Schlager music. The beer is special Oktoberfest beer, brewed exclusively for the event and not available during the rest of the year. But after several litres of it, nobody's really able to tell what they are drinking anyway.

The high spirits and large volumes of alcohol mean it's often a chance for the usually shy German men to try out their best chat-up lines. In fact, Oktoberfest can often be a bit of a singles event. The women wearing Dirndls will wear a ribbon on the left if they're single and a ribbon on the right if they're in a relationship, making the process of working out who is worth chatting up a fairly efficient one. Everything becomes even raunchier in the second weekend of Oktoberfest (or 'Italian Weekend' as it is known) when thousands of Italians make their annual pilgrimage across the Alps in the search for Teutonic love.

Along with the fine German beer, there are also street foods like Bretzels (pretzels), Weisswurst (white sausages), and Obatzda (a Bavarian cheese spread) to try, as well as boozy attractions to enjoy such as Ferris wheels, haunted houses, roller coasters, and other gaudy fairground rides.

A popular gripe amongst Germans is the cost of a Maß of beer, which goes up in price every year. Still, it often feels like a bargain for the millions of visitors who visit Oktoberfest every year. Na dann mal Prost!

56
GET SINFUL DURING KARNEVAL (FASTNACHT)

If you live in the Catholic regions of North-West Germany, Karneval (or the fifth season) is one of the key events in the German calendar. Karneval season officially begins on November 11th and goes right through to Shrove Tuesday the following year, although the majority of the festivities take place around Rosenmontag (Shrove Monday) where there are big parades in the Karneval capitals of Düsseldorf, Mainz, and Cologne.

The main festivities begin on Weiberfastnacht (Fat Thursday), the Thursday before Ash Wednesday. The biggest parades take place on the weekend preceding Rosenmontag, the day that proceeds Shrove Tuesday and on Shrove Tuesday itself. Life, at least working life, tends to stand still during the festival week while people watch both indoor and outdoor carnival performances.

Revellers traditionally wear costumes and consume beer in vast quantities: Kölsch in Cologne and Altbier in Düsseldorf (and never the other way around). Fuelled by equal doses of both beer and feminism, the women arm themselves with scissors and wander around the festival cutting off men's ties (a symbolic castration of the men's status). Traditionally, though, it's followed by a compensatory kiss and the men aren't left feeling emasculated for too long. Karneval is essentially one big week of feasting, drinking, singing, and doing everything but abstaining which begins on Ash Wednesday. Karneval even has its own battle cry; people in Cologne shout "Alaaf" while those in Düsseldorf and Mainz shout "Hellau".

As the Karneval draws to a close, the organisers parade several Nubbels (giant straw dolls) through the streets. These are then burnt at the stake to atone for all the sins committed during Karneval, a clever combination of both Catholicism and German efficiency that ensures you can do what you want for a whole week and still get into heaven.

57

BE TOTALLY INDIFFERENT ABOUT RE-UNIFICATION DAY

One of the happiest days in the German calendar is October 3rd or Reunification Day, the day that the wall came down and East and West Germany re-united. We've all seen the photos and videos: families who hadn't seen each other for decades, hugged and cried in happiness, and the whole country came to a halt as there was nothing to do but celebrate.

These days October 3rd is a surprisingly quiet affair, and the celebrations are low key, at least in comparison to national holidays in other countries for example: the 4th of July in America, Bastille Day in France, or St. Patrick's Day in Ireland (or again, America). There are some parties in Berlin, and in a few other cities, but you won't find many parades or see many fireworks displays. It's something that's changing, as Germans grow more comfortable celebrating their identity, but in reality it's still fairly low-key. Aside from the shops closing for the day, it's easy to not realise it's happening.

Most Germans just enjoy Tag der Deutschen Einheit as a day to relax in front of the TV, head off on a hike with their family, or maybe even enjoy a short holiday. National pride really only comes out during the World Cup and Eurovision, and even then there are plenty of people that refuse to take part in anything that could be considered even remotely patriotic.

58
TERRIFY YOUR CHILDREN ON NIKOLAUS

The 6th of December is Nikolaus, a day when German children leave shoes outside of their door for Nikolaus to fill up with sweets and gifts.

That's only if they've been good, of course. If they've been bad, they'll wake up to find a lump of coal in their shoe compliments of Knecht Ruprecht (Farmhand Rupert). According to folklore, he asks the children if they can pray. If they can, he rewards them with seasonal foods and treats like apples, nuts, and gingerbread. If they can't (or don't want to) he beats them with a stick and a bag of ashes.

As frightening as Rupert sounds, he's nowhere near as scary as the Krampus, a truly terrifying devil-looking figure traditional to Austria but also common in parts of Southern Germany (particularly Southern Bavaria).

On the 6th of December, men dress up in Krampus costumes and go door-to-door looking for badly-behaved children. More specifically, they're looking for the badly-behaved children that they've been paid to visit. Yes, for a not-too-small fee (usually around €50) a Christmas Satan will visit your naughty children and screw with their heads a little, frightening them into good behaviour. If the kids try to talk back to the Christmas-demon, they're dragged outside, held upside-down, and dunked in the snow.

Given that the punishment for being bad is imprisonment in the Krampus layer, most children in Germany are extremely well-behaved. It's possible that this terrifying childhood experience plays a significant role in making Germans such conscious rule-abiders in adult life as well.

These days, the German parenting manuals have had a thing or two to say about punishing children for telling fibs or not doing their homework. It seems holding a child's head under two feet of snow isn't an appropriate response. Old habits die hard though, and if you wander the streets of Bavaria on the 6th of December there's a chance you'll get lucky and see a small child that didn't tidy his room promising Satan he'll never break the rules again.

59
CELEBRATE CHRISTMAS FOR A WHOLE MONTH

German winters can be long, cold, and dark. It's not surprising then that most of the joyous Christmas customs we have today come from Germany, for example, Christmas trees (Tannenbaum), gingerbread houses (Lebkuchenhaus), and advent calendars (Adventskalender).

By late August, the shops will begin stocking Christmas products, and by December, Christmas will be in full swing. Advent calendars and Advent wreaths countdown the days until Christmas, and on the four Sundays leading up to Christmas, a candle is lit counting down the Sundays until Christmas.

The highlight of the German Christmas season is without doubt the Christmas markets (Weihnachtsmarkt). Other cities around the world have adopted the custom, but to get the real, authentic experience you should come to Germany. Cities like Berlin, Hamburg, and Munich don't just have one main Christmas market but tens of them. Wherever there's an empty street corner or a small park, you can almost guarantee that a Christmas market will spring up.

The market stalls are usually made up of a combination of craft sellers and food stalls selling sausages and gingerbread, and depending on the size of the market, you'll often find funfair rides and ice skating as well. Most importantly, it's a chance to drink lots and lots of Glühwein (warmed wine mixed with cinnamon, lemon or orange peel, star anise, and cloves) or Feuerzangenbowle (Glühwein mixed with rum).

Then there's the big day, the 24th of December. The tree is brought out from its hiding place and decorated with apples, sweets, tinsel, and lights. Usually, these are fake lights but Germany still has plenty of die-hard traditionalists who prefer to light real candles instead. This is usually mother's job along with being tasked with the responsibility of preparing plates of cookies, sweets, and baked goods before ringing a bell (known as the Christmas Bell) to let the children know that they can come in. It's traditional to then gather around the tree and sings songs together, Von Trapp Family style.

Germans often refer to the 24th as Dickbauch (fat stomach), which is a good name for it considering the amount of food that gets eaten.
The Christmas dinner is traditionally turkey or goose but sometimes rabbit, accompanied by apple and sausage stuffing, red cabbage, and dumplings. Then there are all of the baked goods such as Plätzchen (cookies), Lebkuchen (gingerbread), Christstollen (stollen), Früchtebrot (fruitcake), Förtchen (a type of pancake or doughnut), Zimtsterne (cinnamon cookies shaped like a star), Spekulatius (spicy biscuits), and Vanillekipferl (almond or hazelnut biscuits).

On the 25th and 26th, most people meet up with family and friends to continue exchanging presents and eating Christmas foods.

60
SLIDE INTO THE NEW YEAR

While the rest of the year is a fantastic opportunity to see German stereotypes like efficiency, rationality, and clear-mindedness in action, New Year's Eve (Silvester) is a chance to see them flouted.

Germans tend to get pretty excited during Silvester, blowing off almost a year's worth of steam in the process. Considering this usually involves holding a beer in one hand and a firework in the other, things can get a little dangerous. Although most cities will have regional fireworks displays, a lot of Germans prefer to take more of a DIY approach. A combination of both giddiness and alcohol means it's not uncommon for fireworks to be set off horizontally and to go flying into crowds of terrified onlookers, or into the air at an angle, zigzagging off the neighbours' windows on the way up.

Even if it's pouring with rain, you'll still see Germans outside trying to light their fireworks, although this is only partly for their love of fireworks, and more because German law states that all fireworks must be set off by the 2nd of January.

Before the pandemonium that is homemade German fireworks displays begins, there are a few annual traditions to take part in, starting with the lead-melting ceremony (Bleigiessen). Every year Germans melt lead and drop it into water. Once the lead forms into a shape, Germans read it to predict what's going to happen that year: a heart could mean that love is on the horizon, while a car or ship means you'll be travelling soon (and that you had better get booking those flights to Mallorca). Bubbly surfaces mean you'll be coming into money while a broken shape predicts bad luck. Of course, in reality it's all down to individual interpretation.

Don't worry if you don't have any lead lying around. In the weeks coming up to New Year, the shops will sell kits containing melting lead for exactly this purpose.

Next, it's traditional to watch Dinner for One, an 18-minute long British comedy sketch from 1963, about a ninety-year-old lady celebrating her birthday with several imaginary guests, and her butler who has to drink on behalf of all of them. Many Germans, particularly those who have been watching this show all their lives, like to join in the fun and take a drink whenever the butler does. Speak to anyone from England about Dinner for One and they will probably shrug their shoulders. Nobody in Britain seems to have seen this iconic sketch, but everyone in Germany has, often several times each New Year's Eve.

And then there are the Berliners. Everyone gets stuck into jam doughnuts, or mustard ones if they're unlucky. There are also plenty of other festive foods like Raclette, fondue, and, of course, plenty of beer and sparkling wine.

As the New Year bells chime it is traditional to wish each other "Guten Rutsch": a good slide into the New Year.

EPILOGUE

Hopefully, you've enjoyed learning about what makes German people tick, as well as a little bit about the foods, drinks, and festivals that are so important to German culture.

Germany is a fantastic country. One that welcomes people from other countries with open arms, and especially welcomes people who have an interest in Germany and what it means to be German.

If you haven't already been, take the time to visit Germany or even come and live in Germany for a little while and see this friendliness first hand. Just remember: don't make noise on a Sunday!

Or cross the road when it's a red man.

Or drink Kölsch in Düsseldorf.

Or be late.

Or make Nazi jokes.

Or pee standing up.

Don't worry, Germans are really friendly people! Honest!

ACKNOWLEDGEMENTS

With a special thanks to Alina Dudek, Jemma Porter, Heidi Becker, Horst Becker, Les & Mary Cave, Sónia Margarido for their feedback and comments, and to Will Dinksi and Bruno Santos (Mantraste) for the cover design.